A Holy Kaleidoscope

A NOVEL BASED ON A TRUE STORY

ANNIE BLEST

WESTBOW
PRESS®
A DIVISION OF THOMAS NELSON
& ZONDERVAN

WestBow Press books may be ordered through booksellers or by contacting:

WestBow Press
A Division of Thomas Nelson & Zondervan
1663 Liberty Drive
Bloomington, IN 47403
www.westbowpress.com
844-714-3454

ISBN: 979-8-3850-1147-6 (sc)
ISBN: 979-8-3850-1148-3 (e)

Library of Congress Control Number: 2023921011

Print information available on the last page.

WestBow Press rev. date: 11/28/2023

Contents

Foreword

There are stories, and then there are testimonies. What an incredible testimony this book exhibits of a life learning, growing, and trusting in the faithfulness of God. "The Lord is the one who will go before you. He will be with you; he will not leave you or abandon you. Do not be afraid or discouraged" (Deuteronomy 31:8, CSB). In this book, you will witness a firsthand account of God's faithfulness amid hardship, difficulty, and unexpected tragedy. Annie Blest knows what it means to walk through heartache and to come out the other side with a heart on fire for God. She is not a superhuman in touch with an unknown deity. Rather, she knows Jesus, and it is Jesus who has developed her through every up and down of life. Jesus makes a promise that if you have the faith of a tiny crumb—the size of a mustard seed—your faith will be grown by Him.

There is not one person who does not need to grow in their faith in Christ. This book is about redemption even through some of the greatest challenges we may face in life. Weakness and hardship are part of everyone's story. But what is it that makes Blest's story different? The apostle Paul put it this way: "In the same way the Spirit also helps us in our weakness, because we do not know what to pray for as we should, but the Spirit himself intercedes for us with inexpressible groanings" (Romans 8:26, CSB). In our weakness, Jesus intercedes on our behalf. It is the spirit of God working through our weakness that enables Christ to be made known to us and to others through us. Blest's journey contains many moments of heartache, but the triumph in her story speaks louder than the hardship.

As you look at your own life, maybe you too have been tormented by alcoholism, encountered workplace harassment, experienced spousal abuse, unable to break through grief, discouraged by low self-esteem, or recognized your need for salvation. This book is especially for you. Even if you have not experienced some of these circumstances mentioned, you know someone who has, and her story provides necessary insight to walk alongside someone who is hurting.

Everyone is seeking, everyone is hurting, and everyone has questions. This is why literature like this is fundamental. With Christ, victory is never distant, nor is it ever impossible, something every person (even much more the follower of Jesus) must be reminded of. As the darkness of the world is ever increasing, those in Christ have a story to share of His marvelous light. Blest's story of a life well-lived demonstrates just what this looks like. My prayer for you as you read the chapters of this story is that you will be renewed in many areas of your life. First, I pray you will be encouraged if you are walking through darkness in your own life. I pray you will be reminded that God certainly has not left you nor forsaken you. "I waited patiently for the Lord, and he turned to me and heard my cry for help. He brought me up from a desolate pit, out of the muddy clay, and set my feet on a rock, making my steps secure" (Psalm 40:1–2, CSB).

Let this book serve as your reminder that God will pick you up out of the pit. Blest's story does not just display the faithfulness of God for her alone, but also the faithfulness of God for all who trust in Him. Secondly, I pray you will be encouraged if you have been through darkness in your past. As Blest so graciously put it, we all have a story to share, so "may we all be bold in sharing the Light we have." Your story of God's steadfastness in your life is meant to be shared so that others may experience the same hope you have known and continue to know today.

Only Jesus can bring you up out of the pit and keep you until the day He returns. Until then, let us live a life worthy of our calling, boldly proclaiming the truth of Jesus Christ. Praise be to Jesus that we have a redeemer who lives and who is on the throne today! May you be blessed, and may you trust the Lord all the more as you grow closer to Him. He is worthy of our worship, He is worthy of our praise, and He is worthy of our life surrendered to Him.

In Christ,
Dr. Michael Gossett
Lead Pastor of Green Acres Baptist Church

Acknowledgments

While a novel contains the creative imagination of the author, this one is also based on a true story. All names have been changed to protect the privacy and confidentiality of the characters.

The Lord supplied the desire for me to write a book and the strength and ability to follow through, so my most profound thanks go first to the Lord, Jesus. Any success the book may enjoy is *all* glory to Him.

I can thank many important people over the span of my life, which this book pretty much covers. You are giants in my life. Family, friends, brothers and sisters, and mentors. The Lord knows your names. Better yet, the Lord knows a more fitting descriptive word for you than *giant*. His is an unlimited language I cannot wait to hear and hope to use! On this side of heaven, let me thank you from the bottom of my heart, for loving me, believing in me, and saying yes to the Lord, to be His servant in ways that profoundly affected my life.

I want to thank my longtime pastor, who says yes to the Lord better than anyone I know. This is the person I will most need those new eternal words to express my gratitude. He has taught, discipled, mentored, tolerated, and loved me as only a pastor can do who is sold out to Jesus. I have also been blessed to call him friend. No person has influenced my life more than this precious man.

Thanks to the wisest woman I knew, now with the Lord, who was a saintly mentor and loving friend, following her calling to love and disciple those in her path without judgment. The Lord used her example of living to speak volumes to a sister in need of all she could give. I could never possibly repay her, but I thank her that I learned to pay it forward.

My Bible stories partner, who loves and invests in friendship in extraordinary proportions. As a result, the Lord used her faithfulness and trust in Him to offer counsel at crucial times.

My oldest, most faithful friend today, a true sister in Christ who has held my hand, loaned a loving shoulder to cry on, encouraged for decades, and has been a vital inspiration in writing and painting.

My missionary friend in Uganda, whose work has greatly inspired my priorities. Her influence and friendship are treasures.

Ben's church family, who will always be mine as well. They breathe unconditional love through a depth of biblical understanding, which is uncharacteristic of many churches today.

My present church family—wonderful brothers and sisters who held my hand through the loss of Ben and completion of the book.

My current pastor, Dr. Michael Gossett, who is one of a kind. Ben told me he was amazing, inspired, and would be used mightily by the Lord in days to come. As usual, Ben was right. I hunger for his messages and will forever be grateful for his part in this book.

My grandma prayed for me throughout my childhood and passed while I was in college. She never got to see her prayers answered, but her hope was in Jesus, not me. I believe she *knew* she would see me again. I cannot wait to thank her!

Peter and Hanna, for your love, respect, and continuing ability to far surpass any expectations I might ever have had of my children. You are the apple of my eye, not unlike how we are all the apple of our Lord's eye (Zechariah 2:8). That's Bible-speak for "I could not love you more! No one with skin on is more important to me."

May He bless all of you as *only* He can. You have blessed me beyond my ability to express adequate gratitude.

For Peter and Hanna

Prologue

All of God's promises are true *all* the time. Each of us is His story living out His promises. Totally unique! Life here is only the beginning—the birth of our eternal life. Birth is not easy. But it is precious life and is glorious in Him.

I tell a story of redemption.
The Lord is the redeemer, and I'm a storyteller.
A Holy Kaleidoscope is our story.

Let the redeemed of the Lord tell their story—
those He redeemed from the hand of the foe.
—Psalm 107:2

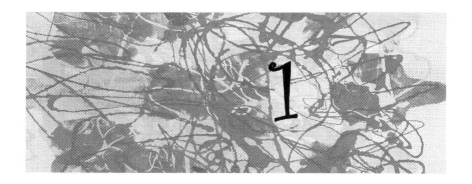

The Getaway

"Hit the deck!" I shouted.

Hanna and Peter would dive to the floor of the backseat. Hit the Deck was the name of the game we played while driving, a pitiful substitute safety measure for an old car with no seat belts. The kids had to stay put until Grandma or I called, "All clear." We practiced and practiced. Who got to the floor first might have been important, but the laughter that followed was always the best part. They never tired of the drill; we played it endlessly. Practice even included rude awakenings from a nap to scurry like little soldiers into their foxholes. Not so much laughter then, but even at their tender young ages, they understood that the underlying reason for the drill was serious stuff on the lengthiest road trip of their lives.

Icy roads stretched 1,093 miles over the course of our 1,700-mile trip from Erie to Albuquerque in January 1975. Two-thirds of the journey was terrifying. The ice storm just ahead of us was slow-moving, but we were even slower. The *we* on the journey included Mom, Hanna, Peter, and me. Hanna was six, Peter was four, and Mom was sixty. I did the driving. I would turn thirty later that year if we survived.

We were driving my grandmother's huge 1960 Oldsmobile 98 with "summer slick" tires and no seat belts. By the end of the trip, the kids had learned to count to higher numbers than they knew when we started. They made a game of counting the accidents we had passed. The journey took a week; we moved in the same direction as the storm.

Mom and I spoke in hushed tones about the incredible dangers we were experiencing. Fears of continuing such an undertaking bored even deeper into our unspoken emotions with each accident we came upon. The accidents we narrowly missed sent us into our own quiet nightmare of a drastically altered life or one that ended. These fears of disaster were best never voiced in the presence of young children.

My eyes were riveted to the pavement just ahead, frantically searching for a tire track, grain of sand, or snow that had not yet turned to ice. Hands welded to the steering wheel, I strained to sense every subtle movement of the car, especially when the car expressed its own directional preference. My driving effort was so intense, so focused that Mom had to read highway signs for us. Taking my eyes off the road surface for even a few seconds was foolish. But turning back would have been even more foolhardy.

The precipitation continually alternated between snow, freezing rain, and sleet. Short days in early January meant we had to make the most of our limited drive window—dawn to dusk at a maximum speed of thirty miles per hour. We saw very little of sanded or salted roads. Evidently, most counties/cities had pretty much emptied their stores of sand due to abnormally early winter snowfall. Nothing was in our favor! Except the scenery left by all forms of frozen moisture.

As an artist, my eyes naturally frame paintings and photos in the imagery I experience. When we were able to stop driving, the entire world was a magnet of visual hype for me. Nothing escaped the ice. The detail of countless tiny fragile ice crystals coupled with the soft snowy fields holding ice-laden trees painted the message of perfect peace in the midst of chaos. Small towns emerged from sparkling tree-lined avenues, looking like Norman Rockwell had already been there.

Such storybook places to live spoke volumes of hope to a seriously damaged heart. All the clean white snow, the artistry, the newness of the imagery sparked an electric current of awareness deep within—making me profoundly grateful to be alive on a new day. At some level, I grasped that God had put together all the beauty I could see. Intuitively and intrinsically, I understood that something or someone was protecting us. Considerable time would pass before I knew the sovereignty in the hand behind it all.

I didn't know my mother very well, at least not as an adult. Mom had the unique ability to make everyone feel genuinely welcome. And each person was made to feel like they were very special. Her cooking was her hallmark, no doubt, but she went way beyond food. If cooking was the trademark for Mom's hospitality, then friendship was her language of love. Mom and Dad had lived in many places, but in every place they'd lived, they'd made friends. The amazing part was they kept the friends in spite of the distances that resulted with each move. Friendship to them was not a casual thing. They invested time and heart, Dad in his way, Mom in hers—they formed an impressive friendship force. I often wished our family worked as well as their friendships.

Seven intense days in the car with her was definitely the longest and most meaningful adult time we had spent together. She didn't really know me very well either. As adults, we had a long-distance relationship that spanned multiple moves on my parents' part and ours. I had been just twenty years old—in my junior year of a fine arts degree program in Columbus, Ohio—when Blake and I had married. Three days later, my parents had moved to Paris, France. Over the next nine years, they had moved six times, and Blake and I had moved three times. Boeing was responsible for all of my parents' moves. The reasons for our moves were more complicated; this would be my fourth move in nine years.

Until a few weeks earlier, my parents didn't even know their daughter's marriage was in grave trouble. I was the only one of their three kids who had not divorced. Each time we connected by phone, Mom would iterate how thankful she was that one of their kids remained stable and married. I didn't have the heart to tell her otherwise. Disappointing my parents probably contributed to my stalling a decision to leave an especially abusive situation. The phone call they received saying my marriage was in trouble was news that broke their hearts.

Still, they were supportive and compassionate, unprepared as they were to hear such unwelcome news. They offered help.

"I plan to move to Albuquerque just after Christmas, which is only a few weeks away. Timing is important to allow the last 'family Christmas' the children might have. Mom, could you fly here and make the drive with me and the children? I might have left right now were it not for the intervening help of the senior minister of a large downtown church we have attended a few times." I explained his intervention and the window of preparation time he had opened.

Talking about such a serious thing did not make sense while driving under severe conditions. Evenings provided the much-needed relief and opportunity to catch up on conversations that should have taken place years sooner. We decided our only requirement of a hotel was an indoor pool. We sat poolside while Hanna and Peter discharged all the pent-up energy they'd stored in a nine-hour drive. Water meant instant games, laughter, and unconstrained release of high energy.

I marveled at the incredible gift these two children were; they were so bright, best friends, and both had already learned to swim. Uncharacteristic of many siblings, they rarely fought or argued. My own sibling relationships were a stark contrast. Mom poured us each a drink of scotch and water. We talked. This became the routine for the length of the journey.

While we had shared a number of holidays and vacation times with my folks over the previous nine years, discussion topics had been light compared to the situation that brought us together for this trip. Having my mother present provided unbelievable relief and comfort in the car, on the trip, in this new chapter, whatever this was going to be! She had no idea the impact her presence was having. The seriously needed mother-daughter relationship was taking on much greater dimensions to include comforting knowledge I was no longer alone. Feelings of friendship with her emerged that I had never felt.

Mom's best friend, Ginny, was always a fun thought. Their friendship brought warm memories in the midst of an ice storm. The friendship with Doris spanned fifty years and was a tribute to both women. Mom might have a particularly stressful day, and I would watch her unwind on the phone with Doris. What I witnessed was laughter, more laughter, and tears from even more laughter. Or I would sit at a kitchen table in our home or Doris's, party to an old-fashioned coffee klatch, and listen to the two of them share perspectives on politics, prices, shopping, and family history. The topic didn't matter. They would talk through it and find common logic, solutions to world problems, and of course, something to laugh about. Laugh hard! What they might not have understood was I would rather have sat at their friendship table than play outside with my friends. Yes, the kitchen table was the place to be when the two of them were together. Maybe Mom and I could enjoy some of this as adults.

I did not want to divorce. Really, really, really did not want a divorce. I'd lingered in a marriage longer than I might have if my distaste for breaking our vows had not been so strong. In hindsight, my dilemma was less about a personal vow to God and more about a commitment to my own integrity.

My parents had a longstanding marriage—the kind everyone wants and one Blake and I had promised to have. Marriage had been the most important commitment I had ever made. After nine years, I was so heavily invested with children and steeped in marital codependency that the option of walking away was not a tolerable one. Besides, who can just up and leave an orphan stranded? I couldn't, even an unfaithful one—a physically and emotionally abusive one.

Blake's father abandoned the family when Blake was five years old. A year later, he was placed in foster care, then in a private underfunded children's home that was dreadful on any scale. His devout Christian mother was moved to a tuberculosis sanitarium, where she died four years later. Once married, my life mission was to make up for all the neglect, abuse, and damage that had happened to the child/man through no fault of his own. Understanding and excusing his adult behaviors was all part of my job.

So calling this move a separation may have been word games, but it was more palatable. A minister in Erie, whom I barely knew, turned my lights on. A change was not really an option—it was imperative. A change required logistical distance to feel safe and to regroup emotionally. It had become apparent that unless I got a grip on life and tried to get healthy, functioning as a mother might not continue much longer. The moment being a mother became more important to me than being married—the choice was made, the corner turned.

Blake and I weathered huge obstacles as we began our life together in Columbus. We were pretty much alone, both still students. He was in graduate school, and I was an undergrad. He would be a dentist in two and a half more years, and I would be a starving artist in another year and a half. He was an orphan, raised in an institution with ninety others. My family was very small and mostly dysfunctional, with parents on the other side of the Atlantic Ocean.

My younger brother was also in France, and my older sister was married, living in Mobile, Alabama. Long-distance phone calls were rare; iPhones didn't exist, neither did text messaging or picture exchange. The internet was still a dream in the mind of Al Gore. We had no financial support apart from student loans. Relationships were largely limited to student friends. The student years were probably our better years—when we lived on love and believed we could overcome anything.

Mulling over the past nine years was impossible to stop. It seemed I had no more control in a failed marriage than on the icy roads putting our very lives in jeopardy. The parallels were unmistakable. Totally immersed in a victim mentality on one hand yet moving away from the cause, I *was* taking some form of control on the other hand. Were these icy roads and this treacherous trip to be a picture of life ahead, or just today? Was taking this trip running away *from*, or was it going *toward* something? I could only clutch the steering wheel, trying to see through a filmy windshield that threatened to ice over each time the wipers did their job.

I deeply wanted one thing: to get healthy. The very word *healthy* was so overused in my self-talk that continual repetition wore me ragged. But the word paved the path ahead. The hitch was how to get there. A method to attain healthy was as remote to me as jumping into a lifestyle of British royalty. I had no way of supporting myself, much less two kids, with an impractical degree in fine arts, no teaching credentials, and no meaningful work experience. Well, there was a year of elementary school teaching back when teachers were in short supply and a troubled inner-city school district was desperate enough to hire even me.

Ten years later, I competed with a glut of certified experienced teachers in a swollen job market. In short, I had no value to anyone in the working world. My goal of becoming healthy seemed naive at best and downright unattainable when honesty reigned. Still, the ice journey would not have begun if I didn't have hope. A vision of exactly where I placed the hope was totally obscured. Answers would come from out there somewhere on my path to healthy.

The few Pennsylvania friends I had were now in the past. Blake and I had moved often enough that most friendships didn't last more than three years. Moving pretty much severed friendships that were not deep. Childhood experience wasn't much better—Boeing moved Dad each time he was promoted. I knew a sister, brother, and parents in New Mexico. Maybe our little dysfunctional family would somehow become loving and functional since we had all grown up. That was a fun thought.

When the road showed a tiny brief improvement, my thoughts would dart backward. It was the only thing that justified continuing to go forward. I fell in love with a young man who had extraordinary qualities that contradicted his tumultuous childhood. The qualities that propelled him through basic survival and then impressive education were not the same abilities needed when faced with challenges of marriage and family. Neither of us were equipped for the difficulties that lay ahead. The ten years held amazing experiences to include hitchhiking throughout Europe for three months, living in New Zealand for two years, and starting a family. But the decade also contained many disastrous choices that led to abuse, alcohol, deceit, and unfaithfulness.

A vision flashed by of being shoved through a living room window that stretched floor to ceiling in our home in New Zealand, watching Blake turn away so quickly he didn't see the pieces fall. Only his back was visible walking out of the living room headed to our bedroom to sleep off the alcohol. My detested memory of a three-second event stalled in agonizing slow motion. This was the consequence for pressing him to know where he had been for the last three hours when he drove the flirtatious young babysitter to her home ten minutes away.

The windshield wipers wouldn't wipe away unwanted thoughts in spite of how much I willed them to. Pushed downstairs one night six months earlier, even with a visiting family from New Zealand staying with us. Worse than the fall was the huge commotion that followed as suspicious friends tried to come to my rescue. Humiliated, I insisted I'd fallen to make it all go away. But it wouldn't go away even now, not even driving away from my home with questionable intentions of returning. Hit in the face many times for reasons I could not anticipate, made for ever-present anxiousness.

One day, a friend called to tearfully confess she had just ended a yearlong weekly affair with my husband. The purpose of the call— she wanted my forgiveness and that I should know the arrangement was over. I knew of other affairs, but this one sent me sliding down the kitchen wall into a heap crouched next to the dangling telephone.

The damage done with his mouth would ring loud bells in my head forever, or so it seemed. Words were worse than the physical abuse. Countless lies, the hammering accusation that I was sick mentally, the vulgar name-calling, cold stony silence for days, jokes told to others where I was the brunt of his fun. The most wearing was the unrelenting lasciviousness in most topics. My objections one night six weeks earlier mixed with way too much alcohol resulted in escalated physical abuse. I was convinced he would soon kill me.

The next day, I sought help in the downtown church we had occasionally attended. The senior pastor didn't know me but listened well. He saw more than enough physical evidence of abuse. When I left his office, he walked a couple of blocks to Blake's dental office to say a few words. Essentially, he intervened on my behalf.

In no uncertain terms did Blake understand that this highly respected man was capable of what he threatened—that Blake would never practice dentistry again if he laid a hand on me in the next few weeks. He explained that I did not want to steal the coming Christmas from the children and needed time to make arrangements to move to New Mexico in the first part of January for a separation. He would be counseling with me three times a week in the interim. While all this happened, I went home to call my parents to break the news that my marriage was essentially over, at least as it was.

Glancing in the car's rearview mirror was just as scary as what was visible ahead. At any moment, a truck or car could slam into the rear of us, challenged by the same inability we faced every second—to stop when we wanted to stop. Not lost was the relatively small size of the rearview mirror versus the size of the big windshield. Past versus future. I knew the past was just that, past. Somewhere down the road, it would make more sense, but never could it be the focus of my life. It had to be a reference for the journey ahead. It couldn't terrorize me, it couldn't consume me, and it could not be denied either.

Thoughts and feelings were not far apart as the car was moving on adrenaline as much as gasoline. Even I realized the thoughts were only goals, not today's reality. For now, in spite of my very best efforts, my emotions were like Old Faithful poised to blow. All energy went into stuffing them, to function as a responsible mother. The only focused purpose in my life was that I loved my children. I poured all of myself into being the best mom possible. If I could fix my mind and eyes on just this one thing, maybe I could make a new life for all of us. Being the mother of Hanna and Peter was a gift. And they loved me. They did not deserve what was happening.

All these huge questions, big thoughts, fears of what was ahead swirled in my mind as though they had to keep rhythm with the blowing, howling wind, ice, and snow. Now, I wondered if God even knew that the storm of the century was raging. If so, why would He let us get through it when hundreds of others met really bad outcomes? How on earth had we made it so far on summer-slick tires? Answers to all my questions would have to wait. For the moment, I only had to know a responsible mother needed to remove children from an abnormal, unhealthy home. The storm was brutal, but the home we left behind was worse. It was all relative.

New feelings were emerging. Welcome relief! I began to feel grateful for the monster storm in a number of ways. We had made it over one thousand miles against highly unfavorable odds. My feelings of gratefulness were enormous. A deeper mother-daughter relationship was developing, and Mom was getting to know grandchildren she really didn't know before the storm. Hanna and Peter's attachment to their only grandma was definitely budding.

The icy journey had been such a consuming distraction for all of us that emotional consequences of breaking up the family had been temporarily forestalled. Hanna and Peter loved their daddy very much. They had not witnessed the dark side of the marriage—I was grateful for that! The drive might have been very different indeed had it been an uneventful, boring long drive leading to children's hard questions I couldn't begin to answer for myself, much less for them.

And then, dry roads. Amarillo, Texas. Just like that. Partly cloudy skies, even some sunshine! Oh my, it felt like a whole new world opened up, which it had. I was breathing once again, no more "hit-the-deck" routines, the car was moving at sixty-five miles per hour, and laughter filled the car. We talked about something other than the weather, the terrible roads, last accident, and how far we might get that day before we had to stop for the night. Maybe, just maybe, the worst was really behind me.

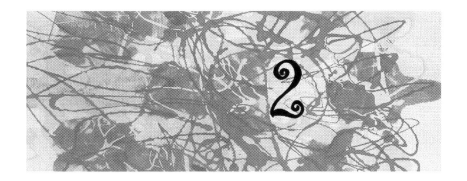

Albuquerque Reality

Bill was the big guy in the back room, the man who owned the business. I hadn't actually met him, but I came to know *of* him quickly on my first day of work. He hired and he fired—a lot of both. Bill made all the rules. Billie Bob, his son, carried out the orders. Bill's baritone voice boomed frequently over the intercom while each counselor worked in their own small private office, putting a very short leash on my newly employed neck. He spoke in code each time we heard him. The code language told all counselors that (1) a new job order was found, (2) a job order closed, and (3) an applicant had been hired.

People were most anxious to meet me. They believed I was their path to a job. It took very little time before I could feel like I was doing something meaningful. Well, actually I was. Helping people get a job and an income was a good thing. If only the *how* part felt good, or I felt qualified for the counselor title, or the income were not 100 percent tied to my job-placement success. The one thing I had to do was find my people jobs who anxiously waited for hours in the reception area. Bill's rule—the applicant could not go home until the counselor found them a job. And that was exactly how I got my first job! They could not place me so they hired me.

Bill's business model perpetually fished for job openings, the unemployed, and new counselors. My counselor failed to find me a job. After two seven-hour days of working/waiting, they hired me. I was so job hungry, lacking in personal confidence, financially needy, and ill equipped for meaningful work in a recession job market that Bill's formula made an ideal catch for him when I walked through his front door.

I barely knew how to write a check. To balance a checking account was a fast-track lesson on how incredibly naïve I was. My skills included drawing, painting, etching, cooking, housekeeping, and best of all, I typed twenty-eight words per minute with fourteen errors. Maybe I could sell my body. How frantic was I? At least I still had a sense of humor. Withholding financial support was Blake's idea of providing incentive for me to return when I got hungry enough. He would send some support, but it did not arrive on a consistent basis so that I could rely on his support for the most basic expenses. And what he sent certainly wasn't enough to live on—I needed an income. To borrow money from my parents was unacceptable to me, and none was offered.

Clearly, I was unprepared to handle what I set out to do. The most important thing I knew with total confidence was I loved Hanna and Peter and would do anything for them. Make a new life—a healthy one for me, for the mother of my children. They deserved at least one healthy parent, and I wholeheartedly believed I was their best shot at having one. There were many miles to go, however, and virtually no road map.

My head ached with bouncing negative thoughts as I combed the want ads in the *New Mexico Daily Sun* just two days earlier. Even a waitress job required waitress experience in the recession of the mid-seventies. Working for Bill was eye-opening at the very least. Most counselors didn't last a month. They did the obvious—grab one of those new job openings we found that came across all of our desks and run. The problem wasn't figuring out the cause of Bill's high turnover rate; I just didn't qualify for any of the job openings we found. Even the straight-commission furniture sales position required furniture business experience. I interviewed for that one and would have been fired had Bill learned.

Lackluster college grades and a bachelor's degree in fine arts with no education/teaching certification made for a pitiful job search platform. The one year I taught school following graduation was in an inner-city school district desperate for teachers amid a nationwide teachers' shortage. An early dose of reality taught me I was completely untrained to handle tough little grade school kids who knew dirty words, disrespected authority, and could smell my inexperience like well-trained detection dogs sniffing for hidden drugs. Classroom management was the name of the game, and the kids were clearly in charge. Undoubtedly, I would have been an interesting observation to a professional teacher, much like when I tried to ride a horse. I was entertainment to those behind me.

Seven years later, the shortage of teachers had changed to a significant surplus of them. Even if I wanted to teach, the door was closed tight. Every other employment door was also evidently closed. So I kept my head down and worked for Bill like my children's next meal depended on me finding a job for the anxious person in the waiting room. It did, so there was no pretending.

The applicant believed I was taking a job application when actually I was taking a credit application. Bill made the credit check call, and I checked their references. The yellow pages were the working bible we used to canvass local businesses related to the applicant's work history for possible job openings. When I found one, I prepped my person in how to interview successfully. After a few weeks, I began to develop rapport with a few of the businesses. If my applicant was hired, Billie Bob took care of the financial side of closure. Employers rarely paid a fee.

After six months, I still didn't qualify for any of the job orders we found in Bill's business, but I had blown way past other counselors in numbers of people placed. I was able to find jobs for others but not myself. My children were eating, and we were paying the rent. I was Bill's little darling, yet he had no clue how much I detested him. He was unethical, greedy, and exploited people at an incredibly difficult, vulnerable time in their life. I absolutely hated that I helped him do something so evil in my mind. The fat cigar he smoked in his dark, dank back office made me gag as much as the visual image of him.

One day, a coworker confided in me, "Did you know Billie Bob is bartering sexual favors on the conference table for job placement fees?"

I quit.

Quickly evaporating was my faulty planning that being near family during such enormous change would be a good thing. Mom and Dad moved to Albuquerque only a year before I moved there. They decided to retire to a place they enjoyed very much three decades earlier in Dad's career. Friends they had in the area had begun a "retirement business" and inspired them to do the same. RoadRunner Travel became quite a successful business. My sister and brother both followed their move to New Mexico within months.

The shared intensity in the ice storm journey that led to a new mother-daughter intimacy level was apparently to stay in the bubble of the car. RoadRunner Travel captured their all-inclusive attention, at least for the time being while their new business developed. They traveled a great deal. The involved grandparent role I had visualized seemed to be on hold.

Mother had found an available apartment for me in the same complex with my sister before our east-west drive even began. An adult-sister rapport began but was rocky. I wanted a sister more than she did, which was pretty much the same status as in childhood. We could not have been more different, but I reasoned the three and a half years between us should be diminishing with adult years.

Diana had a respectable job with Xerox to apply some serious secretarial skills. My job was an embarrassment to discuss; in fact, conversation on most levels with her was ill-matched. Diana finished first in her high school class then magna cum laude in political science at the university level. She was a lifer bookworm. I was socially wired, loved anything outdoors. Domestic stuff was a magnet for me—like sewing, crafts, cooking, children. I read self-help books, not the novels, biographies, and history Diana loved to read. My sister advocated the benefits of alcohol in a failed marriage. That was a path I was only just beginning to discover. Not helping my struggling self-esteem was the fact that she was five inches taller than me, completing the perception that she towered over me in every respect.

Our kids, on the other hand, experienced no reluctance relating. They were practiced at living in the present and made the most of newfound family. The notion that our little dysfunctional family might somehow be loving, supportive, and functional since we had all grown up was nothing more than a naïve desire, wishful thinking. Our family worked a little but didn't in many more ways. I never felt more alone or lonely in my life.

Working relationships with other counselors had led to a few early friendships. People with bachelor's degrees in history, English literature, philosophy, or psychology were nearly as unemployable as fine arts graduates. One of these new friends went to work in a more reputable employment service and beckoned me across town after leaving Bill. Meeting the owner was a sweet breath of fresh air, gentle, confident, and more than willing to hire me despite the signed noncompete agreement Bill required of all counselors.

Ruth put me to work right away and took on the paper battle with Bill to secure my freedom. Within a week, she asked me to manage the business while she gave more time to her husband's dry-cleaning business. She even paid me a small base salary in addition to commissions. This was a catapulting leap forward. But the irony in it all was hard to miss—I was virtually unemployable but suitable for helping others find employment? By all appearances, I was also receiving respect from my new employer. What welcome salve to underlying deep cracks and crevices in self-confidence!

One day, Ruth came into my office accompanied by another woman; they closed the door. Both were all smiles. A few cordial pleasantries were exchanged before they sat down beside each other and stared at me. My nervous index escalated quietly and rapidly, which also served to seal my mouth.

Ruth said to the other woman, "So what do you see in her?"

The answer described colorful auras she saw while her hands drew graceful curves in the air, framing what would have been my head if there were not a desk between us.

"She has a really promising future despite the chaos of her current personal life. Annie is a very old soul, many rich lives. There's been recent violence and running." Kim's words trailed off as she rested her hands in her lap and returned to her silent smile of satisfaction.

My boss knew *nothing* of my days before Albuquerque, but I gawked at her as though she did and she had betrayed me. I had only known this incredibly strange person named Kim for three minutes. Ruth returned my stare and calmly smiled. I could not even blink.

This was the first of more startling educational adventures to come. Things were happening for which no apparent logic or reason could explain. I wanted to know more. Someone knew way more about the past and future than I did. A future that was evidently good! Wow! My negative thoughts were turning positive. This was hope! What was there not to like about this?

Thoughts of reincarnation fascinated me as Kim told me about my past lives in Asia. The writings of Edgar Cayce were some of the most compelling that told me more. The further I pursued the possibility of reincarnation and karma, the more it made sense to me. Perhaps these were the answers I was seeking. Surprisingly, a little research showed I was in good company. Some remarkable people embraced the beliefs like Benjamin Franklin, Henry Ford, Rudyard Kipling (a favorite poet of my dad's), Socrates, Plato, Dante, Ralph Waldo Emerson, Henry David Thoreau, Albert Schweitzer, and George Patton.

In addition to seeing auras around people, Kim was skilled at using tarot cards, speaking with spirits, and focused meditation for insights or revelation about past and future. Her abilities gathered attention, and soon she had something of a following. As I embarked tentatively in this new direction, I discussed newly emerging thoughts at the dinner table one evening while visiting with my parents. They were not as enamored as I was. They were completely unimpressed with my reports of Kim. In fact, my father was particularly displeased that I was dabbling in the Eastern religions.

My argument that belief in reincarnation could fit right in with Christianity was met with an emphatic dismissal, making me feel very misinformed, almost childish. Dad may not have been a classic church-attending Christian, but he was a godly man in many ways, ethical, and lived life consistently to high moral standards he held from a faith-based childhood. The same standards were expected of his children. I had worked very hard for thirty years *not* to disappoint him.

Religion had been a back burner subject in the home as I grew up. Dad was an only child raised Southern Baptist in Raleigh, North Carolina. Grampa was a deacon in the church, and Grandma headed up the children's education. His parents had their son's future all figured out and knew the perfect girl he should marry—she lived only three blocks down the road. By the time Dad graduated from engineering school in the Great Depression, he left North Carolina, the church, and his parents' dreams that he would follow in their footsteps. Making an impact in the world in the newly emerging arena of aeronautical engineering became his consuming pursuit.

Mom was raised on a homestead ranch in central Montana—no plumbing, no heating, and no electricity. Church was infrequent because their location was remote, but she told stories of a grandfather who lived with the family for a few years. He mesmerized her with lengthy biblical recitals of memorized scripture. Her mother marched in the Women's Christian Temperance Union, expressing some adamant opinions about alcohol consumption. How Mom and Dad got together was a wonderful story in itself.

My experiences in church were spotty, very seldom Baptist, largely social in nature when they did occur. Rarely did I hear the name of Jesus from a pulpit, even less often at home. I heard

"Goowwwd" from the ministers who spoke in a drawn-out dramatic way that made me think I should feel reverent, which I didn't and didn't know how. Church held little appeal in my childhood—I didn't have many questions. All I knew was that the difference between Catholics and Protestants was as serious as the difference between Democrats and Republicans. I called myself a Protestant.

The relationship between Ruth and this amazing woman was new; it grew hastily. As they became inseparable, Ruth was less available for her job placement business. When her husband began to appear frequently in our building looking for her, it became apparent she was less available in his business as well. In spite of all the drama going on, the employment business was growing, and things were beginning to settle down a little at home. The whole notion of day care that traumatized all three of us nearly a year earlier had lost its devastating grip on us, at least the kids. Not a day passed I didn't long to be home, raising my children with a father who loved their mother.

One Saturday morning, Ruth's husband knocked on my apartment door asking for a cup of coffee and advice. While the kids watched their favorite cartoons, Rick buried his head on his folded arms at our kitchen table and wept. Ruth had left the children and him, declaring she was in love with Kim and would not be back.

"I might know something about trying to retrieve a wayward wife from another man, but how on earth would I go about winning her back from a woman?" Rick managed to say. "Do you have any advice?"

He broke my heart. Comfort and coffee were all I could offer.

The employment placement business dissolved along with Ruth and Rick's marriage. I was back to searching for a job that could support us. I knew a little more about the process, but still came up short on qualifications. In speaking with the employers, I called every day while trying to find work for others, I often lingered on the thought, wouldn't I really like to have the job on the other end of this phone call? Perhaps the thought wasn't so far back in my mind when "HR manager" caught my eye in the newspaper's want ads. I knew I wasn't qualified, but in the description, the pay was listed. Three dollars an hour was minimum wage, and that's what the job paid. I didn't need my sister's smarts to figure something wasn't quite right.

I applied in person. The VP of Operation hired me when I must have answered the questions right…Well, one of them anyway. My answer "separated" to his question about my marital status would seem to have been the only selection criteria that mattered to him. His response of a smile coupled with, "That's good!" was the deal closer. They manufactured furniture, about which I knew nothing. More pertinent, I knew nothing about human resources. My new boss knew it, and I knew it. I also sensed the game was on.

Fortunately, there were two support people for me that came with the job. They knew their jobs, and it didn't take long for them to understand I didn't know mine. Everything I did initially was fraught with errors they were good to find, correct, and show me a better way. Dancing was the only way to explain how subordinates train their new boss in what turned out to be basically a clerical job. We hired the new people, set up files, input payroll, completed many reports, and did massive filing. The terminations/exits were our world as well.

The job was stressful because my learning curve looked like a plumb line. I loved the people I met and wanted to spend time understanding their jobs, how all the others' jobs fit together to make a chair. What happened on the production floor was far more interesting to me than all the repetitive procedural stuff in the front. Moreover, the front office included the continual leering eyes of my boss.

The minimum wage was not moving up—not as long as I didn't respond to the lusty looks. In the beginning, I didn't like myself very much for speculating if that *might* be the case. After a while, guilt feelings faded into trusting my intuition. Managing on so little income was proving extremely difficult. Pressuring Blake to send support on a timely basis had the opposite effect. We had no contract or even written understanding. His response was predictable: "Move back to Pennsylvania." I suspected he also knew that was *never* going to happen.

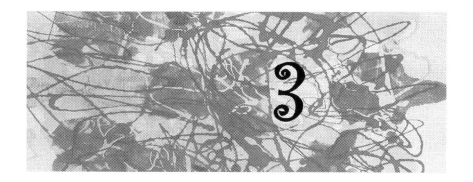

Seeking

The little boy and girl were adorable. How could I not notice them as I walked across the apartment parking lot one Sunday morning in bathing suit with towels and two very excited children in tow? What a perfect family they were! Mom and Dad were not very big either; they were nearly as cute as their children. Father and son in suits, mother and daughter in lovely dresses. They lived just a couple of doors from where I lived in the large apartment complex I called home for fifteen months.

I began watching the perfect little family often. Every Sunday morning, they would climb into their car parked in front of their front door; on Wednesday evenings as well. At first, I thought my attention was drawn to them because they were the perfect family. Self-talk explained my sentiments weren't necessarily jealousy. The feelings experienced were a deep longing and emptiness for the very thing I'd likely never have because I had broken my family, a type of grief.

This perfect little family embodied my most basic dreams, dreams that did a face-plant with separation and probable divorce looming. There would be no perfect family—not for me, worse yet, not for Hanna and Peter, and not for their father either. I had been in Albuquerque long enough to know that the remaining fragments of a marriage looked to be pretty much lifeless.

What on earth was I doing? I had ripped my children out of their sweet little friendships, their neighborhood, all the comforts they knew of a "normal" family life. They knew nothing of the dark side of their parents' marriage, never having witnessed the ugly underbelly. I was working jobs that were more like pretend jobs! Going to the pool or visiting their cousins was great fun indeed, but when that was over, apartment living in a new desert residence without Daddy was very hard for them. Their questions always outnumbered my answers. I couldn't be both parents; it was tough being just one parent, let alone a single parent.

There was no amount of comfort I could provide to Hanna and Peter, diversion of attention, reasoning, or treats offered to compensate for the upheaval I had brought into their lives. They didn't deserve any of the difficulty they were experiencing. When I dwelled on their pain, I felt so incredibly selfish doing what I was doing. What made me so right and him so wrong? I felt powerless to stop the continual cycling through my toxic indecision. In each mental battle, I would try to drive the new thought anchor deeper, my mantra: *A responsible mother takes her children out of an unhealthy, abnormal situation.* The powerful mental rebuttal was quickly returned to knock me back: *So what's the new healthy life look like? And what makes you think you can provide it?*

The new reality had few answers, just overwhelming challenges. A man who was still my husband and would always be the father of my children continued to be my biggest obstacle, even 1,800 miles away. He didn't care if his wife returned to Pennsylvania. He wanted *his* children, like he owned them. To that end, it would seem he felt totally justified in all that he did, which was a lot. First summer into the separation, the children flew back to Pennsylvania for a two-month visit with Daddy. Getting them back took an additional two weeks of near war.

"Mommy! You are going to love the surprise we brought back for you! Aren't they adorable?" Two hamsters huddled in the corner of a small cage, scared out of their little minds. "We already named them," they explained with excitement. Their names were the first and last names of the friend who had called me to confess she was having a yearlong affair with Blake. A cold chill might have stolen the sweet return of my children had I not been focused on beautiful faces.

The second summer was even worse. If indecision, starvation, and my children's emotional pain didn't kill me, the heat in New Mexico would. This was so, so, so hard!

The perfect little family in my new apartment community went someplace more important on Sunday mornings than to a grocery store or on a drive with the kids into the mountains or an apartment swimming pool. The contrast image stuck in my mind like a carefully designed commercial each Sunday morning.

As I inadvertently timed my parking lot presence with their departure, I repeatedly vowed to look for a church and do the right thing—to start taking my two to church. Do what a responsible parent does! But then, so many other things interfered with good intentions. Just what kind of church that might be topped the list of interference. Then a flood of single-mom responsibilities finished the job of interference.

Sometime in mid-February, early in our second year in town, someone knocked on our door just after supper. A precious little boy, no more than seven years old, stood all by himself when I opened the door. It took a few seconds, but I suddenly recognized him as the boy from the perfect family. Up close, he was even cuter than from fifty feet across the parking lot. Whatever he wanted, I was totally prepared to accommodate as I stooped down to meet him on his level. Good thing because he wasted no time on formalities.

"If you come to my church next Sunday, I could win a trip to Disneyland," he said, quite practiced but nervously.

Stunned, dumbstruck! An awkward silence followed as I struggled mightily to overpower the outraged thoughts straining to blast out from my open mouth:

What kind of misguided parents would let their child be used in such a masquerade? What kind of church promotes children going door-to-door to drum up their business? What a dreadful thing to dangle a carrot like

Disneyland so close to a boy who would do anything to get it and will likely never win such a lofty prize! What kind of God would allow this cheap promotional sham get underway for His house?

"What is your church?" I smiled. "And where is it?"

"Oakland Baptist Church!" he almost shouted, all nervousness gone. "It won't count 'less you bring your kids and y'all go to Sunday school too."

That stopped my breathing but not thinking.

I haven't been in Sunday school since I was your age—even then maybe just a couple of times! Not great memories—little tables, little chairs. Grown-ups don't do that! Good grief! You want the whole Sunday morning!

"Well...," I drew the word out for a good five seconds, eyes locked on the cutest little boy face I'd seen apart from Peter's, still thinking but now faster.

I can't say no to a child! Which was the reason I flunked classroom management in Columbus public schools. I'm kinda looking for a church but definitely not a Baptist one. What's one Sunday? Maybe, just maybe the little guy will actually get to go to Disneyland.

"I think we just might visit your church on Sunday." I finally delivered the reward answer.

Business was over just as fast as it started. No goodbyes, he turned his beautiful little face and flew straight home to relay his better-than-fantastic news to parents standing in their doorway watching.

The following Sunday experience was memorable at the least. My kids needed shoes apart from sneakers if we were going to church, I reasoned. So I justified a wild expense I could ill afford. Money was for necessities, not extravagant stuff. No way Peter was getting a sport coat for our first church visit. That would have to wait if my church shopping were successful in the months ahead. At least the search journey was about to start.

Walking through the front door of Oakland Baptist Church was a shock, as if they were expecting us. We were a few minutes late—I hadn't accounted for an overflowing parking lot. We weren't just greeted; all three of us were rushed with huge smiles, outstretched hands for shaking, questions wanting to know our names and trying to help direct us. Warmth, warmth, warmth! Hanna and Peter were ushered away by a small woman barely bigger than they were—destination: children's classrooms, followed by children's church. She assured me they were in good hands and they would be brought back to me, same place, after the church service. They showed eager willingness to participate.

I was taken to a large class that had already begun. Entering from the back, I quietly slipped into one of the few remaining seats on the last row. No one noticed. An hour flew. The man teaching was really good, gentle spoken, articulate, well prepared. Everything I heard was new to me, and it was all about the future. He taught from the book of Revelation, saying some pretty outrageous things, but those were the words he was reading from the Bible.

When he finished talking, I wasn't finished listening. Easily, I could have listened much longer to information that was fascinating. Then he prayed. I had never heard anyone pray like that. He just *talked* to God. Words came from his heart; he wasn't reading. Words of enormous respect for God. His prayer was not for himself, but for others, for the church, for leaders and the nation, for lost people, hurting people. The more he prayed, the more I knew someone was praying for me. I had never thought of myself as lost, but it wasn't hard to figure out that the word fit.

As I stood to quietly leave, everyone in the room stood, and most turned around facing me, nearly in unison. These people must have had eyes in the back of their head! I was swamped. Invitations to sit with people in the coming service came from all directions. Declining them all, I really wanted to disappear. They were making disappearing difficult because they were so nice—many learned my name. They discovered no husband in the picture but two children with me. I lived not too far away and had only lived in Albuquerque a little over a year. I couldn't say any of their names or if they had kids, but finally leaving, I remembered the teacher's name. Brother Green. And I remembered how genuine all that nice felt.

The service was something else. The music was old-fashioned; I'd heard some of it before. Words in the hymns were riveting—quite personal. Same sounds I had heard as a child when we visited my grandparents' church in Raleigh. I liked it and the memories it brought back. As a little girl, I didn't hear a word the preacher said. I was intently watching the entire assembly of women fan themselves in the summer heat while the men sweated profusely in light-colored suits. That was then, this was now. The music was sweet, so were the voices around me who knew all the lyrics.

Pleasantries stopped when the music was over. As I listened to the preacher in this modern air-conditioned church, I began to work up my own kind of sweat. He was yelling, waving his arms and hands, strutting across the front of the church, gripping the big wooden pulpit like we were about to have an earthquake. He wouldn't be still, and he wouldn't pipe down. The thought that I wanted to leave dominated all others.

The hour felt like two or three. Finally, he prayed and the music started. It was over. But wait, no, it wasn't! The song wouldn't end. Over and over, they kept singing the same thing, and the preacher was telling us to bow our head, close our eyes, to consider the most important decision of our lives, to walk forward to the front, confess before others, blah, blah, blah. When I finally broke out of the sanctuary, vowing to myself I'd *never* return, the kids were waiting for me near the front door with the same petite lady.

They made their requests known before I actually reached them, excitedly waving and pleading, "Can we come back next Sunday, Mommy? Debbie and Jimmy, Mark and Sandy are here from our school! And there are others! We started this really cool project this morning that we want to come back to finish! Oh please, Mommy! Can we come back?"

The petite woman stood tall and must have thought she might be needed to advocate their request. "They fit in well and just loved both their Sunday school and the children's church. Will you be bringing them back next week? We would love to have them. They are beautiful children."

The first word that came to mind was not appropriate for church, or children for that matter. I was dying in a squeeze the likes of which a giant boa would take pride to boast. There really wasn't any choice. I reluctantly acquiesced, carefully letting out the words, "Well, you guys, if by next Sunday, you still want to come, then sure—we'll come again."

They were as happy as I had seen them apart from a swimming pool. New thoughts then flooded. *I must be out of my mind to resist this! What more could I possibly want? This is good! My kids fit and are happy! I can do this. Now, I have a week to prepare for that preacher I vowed I'd not see again. The good news is I'd like to hear Brother Green teach again. I plan to open my Bible. Boy, they have this all messed up. Brother Green should be at the pulpit. I'd gladly come back to hear him.*

The kids deserved to have something go their way for sure. A year had passed since "Day Care Nightmare Day," leaving them for the first time. The day was a tornado for all of us. Their faces and cries were acid etching deep marks in my heart. Their pain was something I couldn't take away or even comfort. On the other hand, I couldn't *not* leave them if I were going to make a better life for us. My anger stirred in ways I had never experienced. This was a dilemma and choice I faced solely because of their father. He got all my big anger.

I chose the best day care in town, way outside my budget but so was the cheapest one. It cost nearly double the rent I was paying. What sold me beyond the great references, neat, clean, well-equipped, and staffed facility was the resident St. Bernard who loved the children. Gus was even able to climb the little slide in the playground and go down it! Each day I picked them up, their clothes were covered in the most expensive drool in Albuquerque.

Brother Green didn't disappoint me the next week. The class was warm, the welcome back genuine. Again, I was fascinated with what the Bible had to say. The gifted teacher didn't just stay in the book of Revelation, he also referenced many other passages of the Bible as he spoke, quite a few from memory. Everyone in the class had a Bible. I thought about the one at home Grandma and Grandpa had given to me for my seventh birthday. The prayer at the end of class was so touching and incredible—it brought me to tears.

The church service was such a circus to me once the music part was over. Listening to the man preach was almost more than I could stand. The louder he became, the more I wondered if he actually talked to people the same way. I almost giggled as I visualized him in a Sears store telling a man behind the counter what he wanted in the same manner he was delivering his sermon. Most of the time I spent watching other people as inconspicuously as possible. Families and couples made up most of the attendance although the smaller children weren't there.

The sanctuary was full of nice-looking, wholesome people. What was it about this man that these people wanted to hear? Most of his content was lost, drowned in the volume and visual theatrics. Perhaps because he kept repeating one statement, perhaps because it was the one thing said, not yelled, but when he said, "Don't believe me, read it for yourself in God's Word," the message stuck.

Meeting up with the kids was a total rerun of the first week. The Sunday school project wasn't done and could stretch out for a while. I assured them and the sweet petite lady that we would be back. I learned where I could take the children myself the following Sunday.

My job at the furniture manufacturer was heating up and the salary was so meager I began earnestly searching the Sunday paper for another possible position. How hard could it be to step up from minimum wage? A degree in *anything* had to be worth something. The boss was becoming more than a pest in pursuit of a private meeting.

A drink after work when I got home helped a lot and became a ritual. Cheap wine wasn't hard to find, and the expense was justified. When we were invited to my parents for dinner, they nearly always met me at the door with a quality cocktail. Friends I was making were ready to buy me a drink when I began to commiserate about a pending divorce. My sister's place was always an occasion to have a drink. Everything felt better, more manageable if I could stop for a minute, take a deep breath, and enjoy a drink.

If there was anything advertised that remotely connected with my new HR employment experience, I sent my very brief résumé. It was a long shot—well, more like a Hail Mary, but doing nothing would yield nothing. I tried talking with God like Brother Green, but only once. When I prayed, I felt totally phony. Getting hired in a better job was peanuts compared to the rest of the stuff that must have God's attention. I felt selfish. People were starving in the world, wars going on, natural disasters, and the like. Besides, I was certain God probably thought I should clean up the mess I undoubtedly made.

Brother Green continued to be my Sunday morning drawing card. I took my Bible. He talked about a future time at the end of the Bible that caused me to seriously consider the words coming from a decent man who was becoming credible. The picture he painted of a person's life who didn't know God on a very personal level was gruesome.

The kids loved their time with others, to include play, project, and especially the stories they were hearing from the Bible. It seemed there was no end in sight on the project. Perhaps if I volunteered in their department, we could actually complete the project.

Torture best described the second dreaded hour in church. I considered leaving for coffee someplace nearby and getting back before the kids were released from children's church. Too much could go wrong with that plan. For the third time, I found a seat on the back row in the overly air-conditioned sanctuary and wrapped myself up in the belief that I could stand anything temporarily.

This time wasn't the same. The music resonated as if the songwriter (Bill Gaither) knew I were there.

Because He lives, I can face tomorrow;
Because He lives, all fear is gone.
Because I know He holds the future
And life is worth the living, just because He lives.

I can't sing, but my heart did as I stood gazing upward that morning, words of hope ringing in my ears, tears streaming down my cheeks. There was something so personal about it all—completely surprising and overwhelming. I gripped the pew in front of me inherently knowing I would place my hope in God. I could not have articulated any of this, nor did I have a clue to what steps I'd be taking, but something was stirring within me I could not deny. This was like nothing ever before.

As I sat down, I realized how very little I knew about God. Everyone sitting around me already knew what *I* wanted to know. If I focused my eyes on the hymnal resting in the tray on the back of the pew ahead of me, not on the ever-moving preacher, some of his words might get through.

He talked mostly about Jesus. That was a word I had never understood. In fact, when someone said it apart from swearing, it made me very uncomfortable. Someone might talk to me about God long before I would listen about Jesus. I knew God created everything. He was the Father. Jesus was His son. And they were supposed to be One, tied together with the Holy Spirit, three in One. Or something like that—I didn't get it.

The word *sin* was never used today, so I thought the preacher was really dated. Despite all my cognitive chaos and whatever he was saying, the message came through —Jesus was personal. Jesus was love. He was present. He wanted a relationship with us. Some of this information echoed some of Brother Green's words.

My broken record responses to the kids' persistent questions about when we would be going back to Pennsylvania were not near enough. Not in rebuttal to the tactics Blake was using or things he was telling them. "Mommy and Daddy have huge differences. We don't get along. We need time apart to work through grown-up issues." These and other similar nonspecific and nonblaming answers given to Hanna's and Peter's questions were becoming a joke.

Frequent phone calls from Daddy to his children kept the emotional pitch at home turned up. Most times in which they talked, things would eventually break down to tears, his or theirs. "Why is Mommy breaking up the family?" one of the three would invariably ask.

Blake was desperate. He was no more equipped to recover a marriage gone south than he was to build one ten years earlier. So he became fixed on retrieving his kids, but with little more emotional maturity than a kid himself.

How could I tell them Daddy was unfaithful, abusive, lied, and hurt me? Maybe not even *ever!* Speaking total truth was way above the heads of young children. Seeking counseling was financially above my head. Services for battered women or displaced homemakers would not appear for a couple of more decades. Just like in the old cowboy movies, I wore the black hat, he wore the white hat. It was unbelievably complicated; I couldn't sleep, and I couldn't get rid of the black hat.

"Annie, your husband is here to pick up the children," the director of the daycare said to me on the phone one afternoon. "We don't have him listed as authorized. Is it all right to let them go with him?"

"No way!" was all I could choke out of my paralyzed face.

"He's not going to be happy with that. In fact, he's very upset already that we haven't let him take them. He came all the way from Pennsylvania. The children clearly recognize him as their father," she replied.

Blake was not a model parent. Raised in an orphanage, he had no model. While I had parents, I wasn't from a model home. So I read books while pregnant, self-help kind of books, parenting books, any book that would show me the way. Dr. Spock didn't work for me, but plenty of other good books spelled out the differences between critical and nurturing parenting. Hanna was only a few months old when I found the essence of what I embraced, a writing by Dorothy Law Nolte, "Children Learn What They Live." Hanging the words above her change table, they became my Twenty Commandments of Parenting. I read the words often enough to memorize them.

If children live with criticism, they learn to condemn.
If children live with encouragement,
they learn confidence.
If children live with tolerance, they learn patience.
If children live with praise, they learn appreciation.
If children live with acceptance, they learn to love.
If children live with approval, they
learn to like themselves.
If children live with honesty, they learn truthfulness.
If children live with kindness and
consideration, they learn respect.

Blake's repeated demonstration of "no rules" for parenting in a separation that now extended a year and a half fueled my last step to file for *divorce*, black hat or not.

Rescued

The advances of my boss were tricky to dodge for six months. The company of others provided the needed security for the most part. When I was called to his office, I took another with me. It was unspoken but understood that if I would play the game by his rules, my pay would change. I had other plans—the little bit of HR experience I was quickly gaining might be just enough to get a better job without the unwritten job demands. A search was already underway.

"Maria, my lead on Final Assembly didn't receive the right pay rate in her last paycheck." Matt continued, "It's the second time this has happened, and she's threatening to quit. Can you get Maria's pay corrected today?" The Friday afternoon management meeting ended as Maria's supervisor detained me to request help. Matt had brought production reports, time cards, and paycheck stubs to support his request. We both sat back down at the conference table and dug into the documentation. Once the errors were identified, he got up and returned to the production floor while I made notes for payroll correction.

He was right there in an unguarded second. Evidently, my boss had entered and closed the conference room door at the same time Matt left. The quiet exchange took place at the door not far behind me. He was a short, stocky man; his round red face was mere inches from mine when I stood and turned directly into him. So startled I nearly screamed, my breathing froze along with the rest of me. Without hesitation, he pushed forward against my body with his own, stepping me backward to the conference table, no more than a foot.

The grin on his face was as creepy as the overwhelming feel of his heavy body contact from my chest to my knees. His grip tightened on my back. Quickly pinned at the edge of the table, my thoughts were pure fight or flight. I shoved back hard with my entire being, hard enough to startle him. The instantaneous reaction was powerful and set him off balance for the very moment needed to free myself. Bolting for the same door he had used to enter, I charged out and into the manufacturing floor, not looking back.

Weaving my way through busy people, workstations, pallets of materials, and voluminous unfinished product in various stages, I stayed focused on the door on the opposite side that led to the company reception area. The cacophony of noisy machines and clatter of voices served to buffer the raging adrenaline that moved me without thinking. I reached the other side with very little effort and no interference.

The door to the parking lot was in the reception area. My office was adjacent. All the payroll correction paperwork was still in my hand as I rushed into the refuge of the familiar HR office. I had gripped the paper so tightly that it was pretty messed up. I had to pry open my clenched left hand to turn over the documentation to my wide-eyed coworker.

Few words were necessary to request the pay error be corrected before the end of the day. I grabbed my purse, told both women sitting in HR goodbye, thanked them for all they did, and said I would not be returning. As I walked past the receptionist and out the front door, the relief was so overwhelming I nearly took flight to the car. The final play in the game! It was Friday afternoon, my last day, and I was free.

So why did I want to curl up in a ball and cry by the time I reached my car? The drive across town was especially needed as cool down time to think.

What just happened? Surreal for sure! I never dreamed the twisted little man would carry his repulsive game so far. Big power on his side, compared to my puny position. No way could he have actually raped me in the conference room—so why am I so undone? Blake did far worse to me.

Just because this bully thought he owned me or could do whatever he wanted because he was the big cheese! I'm not the first, for sure! Settle down, you didn't get hurt. You actually got out of work early! What if I report him? To whom? What exactly did he do that was a crime? Besides, he'd lie and deny everything I said. I'd never get another job! Oh no, I may not anyway if I have to use him for a reference! What are my chances of another HR job now!

Ugly thoughts and fears gave way to the finest possible as I turned the car into the best parking spot available right in front of the building. Never had I arrived early at the day care to pick up Hanna and Peter nearly two hours before the usual time. Foremost in my brain was enormous relief—dodging a bullet and never returning to that shooting gallery. It could have gone so differently, so badly.

My hands still shook a bit, but whatever was ahead, we would get through. Worst case, fast-food places paid minimum wage, and I'd work there. For the moment, food service looked like a decent viable alternative. Later, later, later.

This was precious unexpected free time with the kids. To a bystander, it would have been tough to figure which of the three of us was more excited about the newfound playtime we could share. We truly celebrated the moment.

The thought suddenly struck me—this wasn't just any Friday; this was Good Friday. Already I had planned to buy Peter a suit for Easter Sunday despite our meager income. For ten weeks running, we attended the same church. Regardless of where we decided to attend in the future, I knew both children needed to be in proper church clothing. When better to start than Easter?

What's a budget without an income? Even though future income was suddenly outside planning, I had received some support from Blake the prior week. Budget or not, it would be irresponsible to spend a dime before I had another job. *Oh, how much could a suit cost for a five-year-old?* My indecision was stealing our fun. I grabbed Peter's hand and said, "How would you like to wear a suit for Easter Sunday, Mighty Mate?"

He grinned all over when I used his nickname, a holdover from our two years' living in New Zealand. We piled into the car and drove to the nearby mall.

The more I attended Oakland Baptist Church, the more convinced I became that Brother Green should have been the pastor. His teaching mesmerized me and commanded respect. There weren't many of those men in my life. He was such a decent, wholesome man. His prayers were moving. Something was profoundly different and attractive about him, not in a sensual way. He had led me to the Bible, which was full of surprises. The book had answered a few of my questions but raised more questions than it answered. Questions had a lot to do with why I kept going back to this church Sunday after Sunday to Brother Green.

The music, singing, and interaction with others in the sanctuary at the start was the best part of the service for me. Over the weeks, I had to cope with what followed—to tune down the volume and focus my vision on the hymnal in the pew ahead. Some words coming from the pulpit began to take on meaning. Most of what the pastor said presented Jesus at a very personal level. This was a Jesus I really wanted to know and understand. Thus far, this was the sum total of my understanding of what I heard a noisy pastor saying:

> *God and Jesus are Father and Son.*
> *Jesus actually lived here on Earth, 100 percent man and*
> *100 percent God; He taught, discipled, and performed*
> *many miracles.*
> *He came as a love message for everyone, to include me.*

He was killed by His own people in a gruesome death but
came to life again after three days in a grave.
His death was why He came—to save mankind, every bit
prophesied in the Old Testament.
He is the ultimate, perfect, and only sacrifice God required
for everyone's sin, mine included.
The Bible is true, all of it, every word.

Agnostic I was not. I didn't struggle with the existence of God. *Yes, God is the Creator of everything, our Heavenly Father. Yes, He is all-knowing, ever present, and eternal.* This way of thinking was probably a product of my childhood home environment. Dad respected God, so I did. People who struggled with all the "whys" of God were a puzzle to me. If they acknowledged the very existence of a God, then wouldn't their God have to know more than they did or any man for that matter? Their logic seemed terribly flawed to me—they wanted to know all that God knows before they could believe He existed.

Faith and religion were pretty much synonymous. Church was Sunday; when we went, the rest of the week was living the best life we could. Heaven was reserved for the best. My theology was definitely limited; I was biblically illiterate by any standard. But this new picture of Jesus I was gaining turned my head, big-time. I was just coming to see there might be a personal side of God. Jesus was the magnet for me.

The few spoons of Bible food I had ingested made me hunger for a whole bowlful. "Don't believe me. Read it for yourselves in the Bible," the boisterous pastor liked to spout multiple times throughout his sermons. Following his recommendation, I had begun reading some of my Bible.

The concept of evil was something else. I didn't want to dwell on evil—cults came from that! I had experienced more of evil than anyone would ever desire. One result was my maternal protective instincts came fully alive to shield the kids from any more evil, no matter the cost. Comprehending where evil fit in the big picture of

God's design—well, that was tied up in all the "whys" about God, beyond my understanding but not beyond God's. I got that.

I struggled still with weird things that didn't really relate to religion or faith per se. Everyone else in the room knew God much better than I did. They were decent, good people, all involved in some kind of service or activity helping other people, some even with missions in other countries. I couldn't even help myself. They all knew how to pray and where to find the places in their Bible that the pastor referenced as he spoke. They were Christians, and I was a wannabe Christian at best. I was a broken mess. It all added up to the overwhelming fact that I was different and didn't belong.

The Sunday was a beautiful, sunny, warm April day. Easter morning unfolded in slow motion. Both children looked so beautiful to me I could not break free of the visual magic that locked my attention. Why not? The moment was special, good cause to tarry.

Perhaps Peter's new little suit topped with a white shirt and bow tie snagged my extended gaze. Or maybe what Hanna was wearing—a robin's-egg blue Polly Flinders dress with beautiful hand-flocked stitching. Her grandmother gave her the prize dress for her recent birthday—the perfect dress for the perfect little girl. They were so happy, finishing breakfast and giggling about something. I nearly thought out loud, *This moment is so right. This is how life is supposed to work.*

No, the moment was far more. While their appearance was undeniably captivating, my fixation was really about both children. Visual images of them gave me a warm cognitive bath in the present. Thoughts turned to God.

> *God, if You are anywhere nearby, please protect and love them—their future is so uncertain, and they are so very precious. They need a big God and Father like You.*

How could I have been so incredibly lucky as to get these two? The joy of just seeing them happy at the moment could sustain me indefinitely. I don't care about the past or what happens in the future. This moment is the best ever!

What is it about a child's life that is so precious beyond words? They are little packages, totally complete with everything they will need in this life. All the physical systems of heart, lungs, digestive systems, brains, talent, appearance, just amazingly made for their very first day. There is nothing I wouldn't do for them, and they deserve way more than I'll ever be able to give them.

Our trial church experience was beginning to take root. From the children's perspective, not to go back to Oakland would have left significant unmet expectations. I was not so settled. It was true, attending church felt like the right thing to do. It might have been the only thing in my life that *did* feel right. But feeling that *I* belonged here, in this church—well I wanted to, but just wanting to fit didn't bridge the gap.

"Who's ready for big church today?" Bolting out of meandering thoughts, I addressed both kids with my very best energy. "You guys remember there's no children's church this Sunday because it's Easter, right? We all get to sit together! Wait 'til you hear the music! Today is more special than other Sundays."

The kids had never experienced anything like big-church Easter music, nor had I. They were excited before we even reached the front door. Experiencing a church service together, and on Easter, amplified the impact. The choir, accompanied by a small orchestra, sang a medley of grand music partially familiar to me. Surprisingly, the soloists sounded better than many voices on the radio. I had enjoyed classical composers like Handel, even in concert, but not along with voice, not blended with other worship pieces, not where I could participate in some of the singing, and not in the setting of a church. I sensed holiness for the first time in my life.

For the moment, I forgot all my self-excluding thoughts that kept me from belonging as I was fully participating. God touched me through the many dimensions of music! I *knew* He was real. Jesus was alive! This was new—to sing joyfully in celebration along with everyone else! To stand and shout hallelujah, thrilled that Jesus was alive. The expressions of elation all stopped before I was ready to stop.

Once settled quietly in our seats following the music, the children sat perfectly still and attentive without even a parental prompting. From that point forward, it felt as if every word spoken were said directly to me in an unmistakable conversation I had with the Lord himself. He told me He was present today, very much alive, and He loved me *just like I am*—so much that He died for me. He told me His love was different from anything I had ever experienced, a love I could always count on.

The words were beautiful. Hot tears popped up, blurring my vision at the mere thought of embracing them, personalizing the incredible message. Accepting them was something else. As if He didn't really know what a colossal mess He was talking to, I began to explain my tangled desperation. I poured my heart out.

> *Lord, it's just me with two incredible, innocent children. They are depending on me. I'm so lame I don't even have a job. You heard me cry out to You two nights ago in bed, so fearful and terrified I had trouble breathing. They honestly think everything will be okay but, Lord, if I could give up, I would. I don't even know how to do that. I can't let them down, and I can't hold them up. Any moment I'm about to break into so many pieces I'll just evaporate.*

God—"I am going to show you a far better way." (1 Corinthians 12:31, NASB20)

> *I am so afraid, and I ache to the bone with loneliness. My biggest fear is that Blake is right—I will fall on my face and*

have to run back to him. I'm beyond afraid. Please, God, don't let that happen for the sake of Hanna and Peter.

God—"I will take you by your right hand, help you, and you can stop being afraid." (Isaiah 41:13, paraphrased)

I'm soooo very tired of trying. A year and a half and all my best efforts would seem to be for nothing. Everything is working against me. Are You going to help me try harder?

God—"Your ways are not my ways. My power is made perfect in your weakness." (Isaiah 55:8; 2 Corinthians 12:9, NASB)

I'm not even sure if I'm doing the right thing, divorcing their father.

God—"Trust in Me with all your heart and lean not on your own understanding;
I will make straight your path." (Proverbs 3:5–6)

This all sounds much too good to be true! Trusting anyone right now is something I cannot fathom. Loosening my grip even for a nanosecond would be disaster! There isn't a single person who hasn't let me down. I can't even trust myself.

God—"I will never leave you or abandon you." (Deuteronomy 31:6, CSB)

But I cannot even see You. How can I trust You?

God—"You can trust me, Annie, I am your God." (Isaiah 41:13, paraphrased)

I'm not even lovable; thirty-one years is long enough to learn that. I learned it at home, and I really learned it in marriage. I'm not like all these other people. They're good and wholesome. I'm not and I'm all tied up in angry fearful knots, a life of complete bedlam.

God—"Annie, I will heal your broken heart and bind up your wounds (Psalm 147:3). I love you and value you so much I sent my Son to rescue you. He died for you, and you are fully forgiven. Had you been the only one living on Earth, He would still have come for you (John 3:16, paraphrased). My love for you is for more than thirty-one years; it's eternal" (Psalm 118:4, paraphrased).

Totally immersed in the most intense experience of my life, I struggled to transition between words the Lord was saying and words of the pastor. He quoted the Bible continually, so thoughts and hearing were comingled to the extent I was not consciously discerning well between them. Everything said had become totally personal. The pastor was telling a story, reading from the Bible.

The disciples had been in a boat most of the night. All of their efforts were spent just trying to reach the other side. But the winds were against them, strong, unrelenting and the men were making little progress. Just before dawn, they strained to look out across the water at something moving toward them. A figure was coming, advancing from across the top of the water. They were absolutely terrified and screamed, believing it was a ghost. But it was Jesus. Immediately He spoke to calm and comfort them, saying, "Don't be afraid, it's me." Without hesitation, Peter boldly spoke, saying, "Lord, if it's You, tell me to come to You on the water." "Come!" Jesus said. Then Peter trusted completely and got down out of the boat. He walked on the water toward Jesus (Matthew 14:22–30, paraphrased).

The children brought me back quickly when they asked why I was upset. My face was wet with tears in spite of determined efforts to betray nothing on the outside that was happening on the inside.

The pastor was still quoting the Bible, saying the Lord was my Shepherd, Savior, Provider, my Father, Redeemer, Rebuilder, and my Healer. He was pretty worked up, telling me to forget about what I could bring to the Lord. God required nothing. Peter had done nothing to make himself walk on the water. In fact, I would be a braggart if I could even help a little to save myself. He was God, able to do anything. All I had to do was believe. Believe Jesus was who He said He was. That simple—He offered me a gift of grace, His hand. He also gave me free will.

All the tension I was experiencing disappeared as I closed my eyes and answered Him, "*Yes, Lord! I believe You.*"

Music began again like it always did at the close of the church service. The pastor was inviting people to come forward. This was the tenth Sunday in a row I stood listening to this. I disliked this very portion of the service the most. Some Sundays he would continue the singing and beckoning people to go forever—until I would nearly run out. It drove me berserk. But this Sunday, Jesus was inviting me to come to Him.

The pastor was urging people to be obedient to the Lord and confess before others what they believed as the Bible instructs. My feet were glued to the floor, tension building once again. Over and over, they sang "Just as I Am."

> Just as I am, without one plea,
> But that Thy blood was shed for me,
> And that Thou bid'st me come to Thee,
> O Lamb of God, I come! I come!

Just as I am, though tossed about
With many a conflict, many a doubt;
Fightings within, and fears without,
O Lamb of God, I come, I come!
(Writer: Charlotte Elliott, 1836)

I began to fidget. A man and his wife stood between the aisle and me. I barely turned their way, and the woman whispered, "I will be happy to stay here with your children if you are wanting to walk up front."

I did. I got down out of my boat and walked toward Jesus.

Baby Steps

At eight fifteen the next morning, the phone rang. A mining company wanted to interview me for a secretary position that afternoon. Quite certain they had the wrong person, I politely said so. The man on the phone explained the position was titled secretary but would be more clerk-like in nature, in the HR department. They believed my résumé expressed what they needed.

He described a real job. A respectable employer interested in me? Really? The pay was better than minimum wage, also offering paid health care benefits, vacation, sick pay, the works. Convinced this was too good to be true, I further tried to disqualify myself, volunteering that I typed twenty-eight words per minute with fourteen errors.

"I don't type *that* well and am presently doing the job." The man laughed and said he had been there only a few months and was trying to hire his replacement so he could perform broader administrative responsibilities.

"I want a person with a bachelor's degree, though I don't really care about your focus of study. The position will start as a clerical function so I can't commit to a very impressive starting salary."

To me, anything above minimum wage was impressive—this was! Plus, the hint of promotion to something even better made me sit down on the kitchen floor where I had been standing.

"However," he was quick to offer, "I'll review pay and your assigned responsibilities after a short time if work goes well." He spoke as if I were already hired.

The man on the phone turned out to be a Vietnam vet working in a newly formed HR department under the leadership of a sweet gentleman who had been a mining operations manager for years and was nearing retirement. To say he was put out to pasture in the newly assigned HR management position would have been unkind, but I knew more about HR than either of the gentlemen did and what I knew was pitifully little.

To launch the planned expansion phase, the company moved their small newly formed HR department to a leased building near the main facility. Significant growth was anticipated in the near term. The logic was twofold—separate the chaos of recruiting from the rest of business and alleviate somewhat the overcrowded conditions in the headquarters building. The actual mines were 175 miles away. A new headquarters facility and location in Albuquerque were on the drawing board; all offices were to be moved within the next six months.

They hired me because the three of us got along famously. Work began the next day. References were never mentioned. I might have been a Christian for only twenty-seven hours, but even I could see that nothing I did brought about such an extraordinary outcome. The timing was not coincidental. How this could happen didn't even pass a commonsense test. No one gets hired by a reputable company because they have a one-time great interpersonal interaction with the interviewers. The interview was more like conversation at a cocktail party; not much was even job relevant.

My prayer for a job had been 100 percent desperate, 100 percent nonspecific, with puny hope and even less expectation. I would have settled for a beaten-up old VW Bug. The Lord delivered a brand-new Mercedes, so to speak. I just kept staring wide-eyed at the ceiling, saying, *"Thank You, thank You, thank You!"* But blessings were not over.

—†—

My apartment management had notified tenants weeks back that a substantial rent increase would be effective June 1. As I talked within the family about needing to find another apartment very soon, my parents suggested their realtor friend might find a house for little more than I was paying for an apartment. Living in a house once again sounded like a dream, but I couldn't image anyone renting out a decent house for the same amount I paid for a small apartment.

"No," they explained, "you need to *buy* the house, not rent it."

I nearly laughed out loud that they thought someone with zero established credit, earning minimum wage, might be able buy a house. Just six months earlier, I humiliated myself when I asked Dad to cosign the purchase loan of a bed and dresser for me. I slept in Peter's bunk beds for a year because buying a bed without credit was outside my reach. We clearly lived in different worlds, and they had no clue what mine was like. But the Lord did.

At the end of my first week of work at the new job, the realtor friend of my parents telephoned. The mortgage credit application I had completed at my parents' insistence was approved! She had found for us the "perfect" little house. Did I want to see it? The mortgage payment would be *exactly* what my apartment rent payment had been.

"You will need *only* $5,000 as a down payment," she concluded.

"Oh boy, wouldn't we love that!" The realtor knew I had filed for divorce and that a settlement was pending. There was nothing I could do to expedite the process or know what I would have financially until it was done.

"Just maybe! I should know in the next couple of days," I responded quickly.

"Annie, this is an unusual find. It's darling, in a very nice area, and you won't need to do anything but move in. It may not still be available if we wait even a few days." I hung up, asking a very unimpressive prayer. How could I even ask something of a God who had already given me so much? I didn't deserve what He'd already given and knew *for sure* I didn't deserve more. I asked for the sake of my children.

The divorce was finalized a few days later. The $5,000 in property settlement was awarded to me. The little house was everything the realtor said it was, and it was still available. Out of nowhere, it would seem we had a new home. There was no mystery in my mind as to who made all this happen. Countless big and little pieces, good and bad, over the space of considerable time, had to fit together perfectly to put us in our own home at that exact time. Only someone who knew way more than I did, who loved us "up close and personal," who was providing for our needs, who could move mountains, could have made this stuff happen.

The Lord had my full attention and praises that lasted well into the night. Brother Green had said something that stuck for me: "Grace is when God gives us what we don't deserve and mercy is when God doesn't give us what we do deserve." I *knew* I was living in pure grace and full mercy combined.

Wonderful things were happening so fast! Incredibly good things! For the first time since we moved to Albuquerque, the children were showing definite signs of adjusting. Everyone was just happier. I was starting to get a decent night's sleep. Brother Green announced he had been called to pastor a small Baptist church across town—many of us followed him.

A sense of gratitude like never before permeated my heart and mind. I knew without a doubt that I was not the cause of anything good happening—the Lord was showering us in unbelievable blessings. I spouted all over about what God was doing. Everything was *new*! Some of those I told replied with some interest, but my family glazed over. The looks I got said, "This too shall pass."

Life was going to be different and already felt different, not just in the shower of blessings, but within me. While at my parents' home for dinner, I looked at the cigarette in my hand (and theirs) and wondered what the Bible said about tobacco. And the drink in the other, (and theirs)—was that addressed? I was aware Jesus turned water to wine for a wedding, so that couldn't be all bad. How much change was I going to be making to be more like the others I saw in church? I had no words for the thoughts, but I was more drawn to the people I didn't even know in church than the chaos and lifestyle in my small family.

My boss had sustained significant injuries in Vietnam and found that talking about his war experiences was healing. He did so at length. The sweet gentleman in the corner office spent his time talking on the phone with family and friends, planning his upcoming retirement. He also loved telling me the old stories of his early years in mining operations. Mail came to his inbox then quickly to mine with a sticky note saying, "Please take care of this."

My learning curve continued to look like a plumb line, but in this new position, no one was around to train me. The HR physical location was separated from the administrative headquarters by a quarter mile so that coworkers amounted to a boss and grandpa boss. I began asking the Lord to help me in all the ways I didn't even know how to ask. I had just learned in the scripture, "Lean not on your own understanding; in all your ways submit to Him, and He will make your paths straight" (Proverbs 3:5–6). Clearly, I had no understanding of my own on which to lean. Still, the path ahead with Jesus was pretty obscure.

I wouldn't be able to keep the job, much less do well enough to receive a pay increase or promotion that was looking very remote, if I couldn't get through the inbox. If a letter needing response had a phone number on it, I would call—people were usually helpful. Questions always led to more questions. Slick-colored advertising materials for one-day HR training seminars found their way to my inbox. I requested permission to attend some that were local. They helped a great deal.

Notice of a local HR management conference appeared in my inbox one day. My boss was invited but did not want to attend. I offered to go in his place, take notes, and give him a report. The day was a gold mine of names, phone numbers, and invitations to call anytime. Wow! Better than Google.com would be forty-plus years later! Connecting was my ticket through the dreaded inbox and the much needed on-the-job training.

—✝—

Everything seemed to be moving in a flawless direction. The Lord was gracious, kind, and incredibly generous. I was receiving so much for which I hadn't even asked. The pace of everything had picked up, and there was even some order in the chaos. I no longer lived in a state of utter fear and desperation. My hope was now in an Almighty Father, Jesus, and the spirit who was within me. New perspectives were just unfolding. While I was still ecstatic with the newfound spiritual awakening, the unpredictable happened.

Blake moved to Albuquerque. Not unlike if I had been slammed into from behind on the icy highway from Pennsylvania to Albuquerque. What happened? I thought I had reached the dry pavement. On some level, I believed divorce would remove all the pain and anguish that drove me to make the decision to end the marriage. In reality, divorce just exchanged one intolerable situation of pain and anguish for another kind of pain and anguish.

Blake's presence and expectations were constant and tyrannical.

"No court in the land can tell me when I can see my children and when I cannot," he would say to justify his outrageous behaviors outside the divorce decree.

"My love for them cannot be bound by rules," he repeatedly said, especially in their presence. The weekends he was scheduled to see them always went as planned. The weekends I was to have them rarely went as planned. He would often buy tickets to fun things on the weekends they were to remain home and then ask them directly if they wanted to go. The midweek Wednesday visitations were continually changed, and additional weekdays were often needed for things he planned.

One morning, I left for work but forgot something and had to return to the house. The kids were still there; they had a few minutes before they needed to walk to school at the end of the street. Blake was in our home. The ritual had been going on daily for weeks. He would wait around the corner until he saw me drive away. He then told the children not to tell Mommy or she would never let him see them again. They didn't tell. Ending his daily visits resulted in lots of tears.

Not many days passed that some incident didn't occur that put the black hat more squarely on my head. I wanted another divorce. It seemed the first one didn't take, and wine started to taste even better to temper my temper some days when I got home. Work offered a sane avenue to relate to healthy people, engage in things that were appreciated and needed, and escape the growing problems of Blake's presence for a day.

Our church attendance was Sunday morning, occasionally Sunday evening. Time didn't really permit much else in terms of church involvement. The kids were in a smaller Sunday school class in the new church we had joined and attended big church with me since there was no children's church. The service was far more satisfying for me because Brother Green's teaching was excellent, every word nourishing.

I love what the Bible tells of Jesus: "He called a little child to him, and placed the child among them. And He said: 'Truly I tell you, unless you change and become like little children, you will never enter the kingdom of heaven. Therefore, whoever takes the lowly position of this child is the greatest in the kingdom of heaven. And whoever welcomes one such child in my name welcomes me'" (Matthew 18:2–5). The understanding of this passage was wonderful for me.

Hanna and Peter were not too young to grasp what Jesus was about. They were anxious to tell me what they were learning in Sunday school and had still more questions at home. The remarkable blessings we all enjoyed living in our new home did not elude them, and I tried not to miss the many opportunities to credit the Lord. Only a matter of months passed until both children told me they wanted to invite Jesus into their hearts to live.

Six months into the new job, we moved to the new headquarters building. My two "friends/bosses" did not; one retired and the other went to work in a new position at the Veterans Administration. My new boss was a young attorney who knew labor relations inside out. Getting along famously wasn't going to get me very far with him; plus he was as serious as a train wreck. He asked me to write a job description of exactly what I did.

I tried to prepare myself for the worst possible outcome, probably dismissal, when we met to discuss what I had written. So when he promoted me and nearly doubled my pay, I was dumbfounded. As I thanked him profusely, he summarily dismissed my gratitude saying if the company didn't reassign me into the job I was actually doing and pay me for the work appropriately, I could sue them. Pay was moved from hourly to salary.

The serious boss was a tough taskmaster. He would request I write policy and communications I had never attempted. I'd labor and then labor some more before giving him my finest try. I would watch my in-basket like a hawk for his feedback. He was brutal with a red pen. He might as well have slaughtered a chicken all over my best effort. Time and again we went through the ritual, but I learned. He made my former learning curve look horizontally flat.

He pushed me down deep into writing technical job descriptions, recruiting and interviewing engineers, participating with a consulting team engaged to value professional jobs, both hierarchically within the company and externally within like industry for pay purposes.

I visited the New Mexico mine locations on a frequent basis, became involved in employee relations, and served on a benefits redesign task force with the other corporate divisions that required travel out of town, all to say the opportunities and progression afforded a female with a fine arts degree were considerably outside the norm.

Some of the mining operations diehards I had come to know and like decided I needed a hazing-type experience to be truly included as one of them. Melvin Marquez was selected to lead my first underground experience. I thought I was doing a job audit of a party chief surveyor, to follow him through a typical day's routine of mapping out future veins to be mined; I would note all job content observations. They liked me. Looking back, I would have settled for less affection.

My anxiety was only slightly offset by the caring preparation I was given above ground.

"If you wear all the right gear, you will be more than fine," they told me as they put me into water-resistant overalls, a jacket, boots, safety glasses, and a helmet with a mounted light on top. All gear was provided as necessary even in the heat of a New Mexico summer day. Underground would be quite cool, I reasoned. Besides, the clothing was more protective than anything. I certainly wasn't a picture of fashion. The fact that nothing fit me was quickly overcome with a few straps, roll ups, and language like, "Hey, I have to do this on mine too. This stuff doesn't really fit anybody." The prep was done. They handed me a clipboard with attached pen I would need for notes.

Melvin and I hopped into a small, open-sided, cage-like lift that dropped over a thousand feet straight down through sandstone into the company's deepest mine. We traveled faster than I would have driven and didn't stop until we hit the bottom of the pitch-dark mine. In my zeal to look like everyone else, I quickly hopped out into the first lighted area I had seen since leaving the surface. But the lift met the bottom with stored energy. It needed to bounce just as I stepped out. At least a dozen men were standing in the open area to observe far more entertainment than any one of them had anticipated.

The dirt where I planted my first foot was thick muck, reluctant to release my foot before I placed the other foot. My second foot was thrust up and over by the rising cage now behind me to land in more of the same slop. The oversized big boots couldn't handle the overriding laws of physics—two or three steps into the drama, and they were left behind.

Socks only, I finally stopped nearly ankle deep in thick, muddy muck but still upright, gripping the clipboard cradled in my arm as though it had saved me. The oversized helmet rocked downward, covering my eyes. No one said a word as they gawked. Lackluster Melvin handed me the boots and stepped toward a tunnel leading away from the lighted open area into darkness. Mortified and sweating like a menopausal hot flash, I scurried to catch him.

I was noisy as I slurped along in the boots, but the gooey suction inside them helped to keep them on my feet. I couldn't see. The light on my helmet was focused upward, not out or down. All I could see was Melvin's helmet light bobbing along, moving farther away. The back of my ears hurt like the glasses were trying to pull them off my head. That was because someone attentive to detail had shortened the arms, perhaps the same person who pointed the helmet light upward. The coveralls and jacket were much too bulky and heavy, but I had more important things to worry about—catching Melvin.

When his light disappeared entirely, I had to reach the spot where I saw it last and pray I'd see it again to the left or right. Tripping on railroad ties, I threw the clipboard down and took the helmet off to use as a flashlight. Melvin slowed occasionally when a train was coming or if his next turn was too far ahead of me. There was barely enough room to plaster myself up against the dirt wall as a train full of ore didn't slow down one iota. I was invisible.

There's an amazing amount of water deep underground, springs everywhere. It showered down on us as we climbed the ladder up a thirty-foot rise, Melvin nearly at the top as I just began. Cold water ran down inside my sleeves and then to my torso, which was already sweat soaked. For three hours, I chased the man.

Finally, I screamed, "Melvin, stop!"

He did. In a short time, I reached him. Surprisingly, there was a nearby rise and path to a lift.

I know how long the episode lasted because the hairballs on the surface had a betting pool going. No one had ventured to put money on such a lengthy hazing duration. As I surfaced, I received a hero's welcome. No woman had ever been hazed. Most men didn't last that long. Oh wow! The thrill of acceptance waned as I removed the gear, handed off the weighty burden, and felt blood on the back of my ears. I still had 175 miles to drive home before fixing dinner for two children I had seriously wondered if I'd see again!

The boss assigned my attendance to as many seminars as possible. The company grew considerably. I was fortunate to be part of the two-year aggressive growth period. Thus began a meaningful career in human resources, a field unrecognized at the time for an accredited degree. Our work was commonly populated by people with degrees in unrelated disciplines. We learned the ins and outs of HR through on-the-job training, seminars, reading government law, guidelines, and relevant case laws pertaining to people in the workplace. I was blessed to work for an attorney. We learned even more as employees presented unprecedented problems. I learned early the most important thing I had to do—wear a hat as an employee advocate at the same time I wore the hat of the employer's interests. Neither hat could be bigger than the other.

One evening, we hunkered down in the living room with popcorn and lemonade to watch a much-anticipated television program. A ninety-minute documentary on the search for Noah's ark was showing, and we invited a friend I had made to join us. If I were ever to doubt the authenticity or validity of a child's belief in Jesus, the Lord set up what followed to be a marvelous life lesson only a few months after the children decided for themselves to embrace Jesus in their innocent childlike faith. The friend now sharing our popcorn and lemonade had also accepted a couple of our recent invitations to attend church with us. She was a skeptic.

The film was an archeological chronology of numerous expeditions beginning in 1829 to the present day. *Every* mission had failed to reach the ark perched high on Mount Ararat, many with disastrous ends. As the film progressed, so did our friend's anxiety.

Repeatedly, she would impatiently proclaim something like, "Give me a break! How hard can it be to climb that mountain?

People have climbed higher mountains than that one!" or "For crying out loud, this is the twentieth century! What's the matter with those bozos, they can even see where they have to go?"

In utter frustration near the end, she was on her feet pacing with car keys jingling in her hand, threatening to leave before we learned the outcome of the final expedition.

Peter was eight years old at the time. He had been very quiet, really glued to the program with the best seat in the house. He was lying on the floor only a few feet from the TV, chin propped up with his elbows.

"This is ridiculous to watch! Give me one good reason one of those expeditions hasn't gotten to the ark!" my friend finally exclaimed in disgust.

Peter rolled on his side and spoke for the first time, saying to her, "Because God wants you to believe with your heart, not with your eyes, Beverly."

The following Sunday, Beverly accompanied us to church for the third time, making the decision to give her life to Jesus.

My employer got into a huge fracas of complex lawsuits with other larger mining companies over unmined mineral reserves. They fought with everything they had to hang on to their undeveloped assets. Ultimately, they won, but it cost them everything. The company didn't survive. In his position, my boss could better assess the imminent outcome. Telling me what was coming was at some personal risk, but he promised to provide a favorable recommendation. Losing my job was so sudden, quite final, and I was completely unprepared. How could this happen? I knew the lawsuit had been won! Old feelings of fear and desperation washed over me and took hold both day and night.

A *Wall Street Journal* was sitting on my desk. Turning past our ad in the engineering section to the section that might have HR positions, I found a research organization that was in a start-up mode, looking for a technical recruiter. I took the newspaper home, prepared a résumé, and sent a Hail Mary to the employer. Then résumé in hand and a little recruiting under my belt, I seriously pursued any other local employers I thought might have interest in me. Nothing resulted.

Days later, the call came from the research and development organization. They wanted to interview. The likelihood of my being hired with my scant experience and nontechnical degree by a highly technical organization in a start-up mode, was remote. The job represented rich opportunity, significant progression, and increase in pay. They were recruiting on a national level. The position was in Denver, Colorado—they sent an airline ticket for the interview. I could smell a possible God thing in the works.

Divorce No-Recovery

Flashback

Everyone in the classroom knew how to read except me. They were learning to write in cursive; I couldn't even print. They were all strangers to me as well. The first day of school in a new school was always tough, even in the second grade; mine was January of 1951. The word *dyslexic* was not known, at least to anyone in the room or my family.

Dad got a new job, an important one that would move us across the country in the middle of a school year. I was the new kid from New Mexico to these Ohio classmates. At the age of seven, they stared at me, believing that I was from another country like Mexico, the concept of states and countries not yet fully learned—one more thing to set me apart.

Day two in the classroom really set the pace.

"Annie, would you please stand and read aloud beginning at the top of the page?" The teacher startled me from an immersed fog as I sat observing my surroundings. I stood utterly terrified with the open book, unable to say a word in the lengthy silence that followed. The whole class heard my tinkle hit the floor before they erupted in laughter.

In retrospect, a curious thing happens to a kid who is identified as slow at reading. Very soon, the child is thought of as slow at *everything* in the culture of grade school. Several decades later, I would come to understand a much bigger picture of reading problems, but that was little help during those important developmental years.

In high school, I caught a break—an event occurred that would change the course of my life. The summer I turned sixteen, my reading speed went from fifty words per minute to five hundred in the course of a six-week speed-reading class offered at a local university. Most students in the class were not slow; they were learning to speed-read. I was learning to read.

A light moved from left to right on a big screen filled with words. First, just one word, then a few words, then a whole line, then many lines flashed on the screen. Over a period of six weeks, the light trained my eyes to sweep from left to right versus the chaotic hopscotch method that moved my eyes every other direction in completely unpredictable ways. This class was a game changer.

Normal was a brand-new feeling. Average was a beautiful word! No longer slow! Like others, I could read! I was like everyone else. To describe as euphoric what the *new* me felt like would have grossly understated my feelings. No more trying to fake it. No more horrifically embarrassing situations. For a time, I was nearly airborne with what felt like unshakable confidence.

My self-esteem at the age of sixteen was no better than it was on "Crater Day" in second grade. Since that day, I labored like a puppy locked on a rag to *look* like everyone else and hide the unintelligent girl inside. Hard work paid off—I had become surprisingly accomplished at concealing much of a pitiful self-esteem, largely camouflaged in social adeptness. I became a cheerleader, was fun at parties, dated, and socially thrived in a small high school class of only seventy. The very facade I labored to build made announcing the *new* me self-defeating. So I did not.

Euphoria was short-lived. Within days, I figured out I was just as "slow" as the family perceived me to be, and friends didn't change their perception of me just because I could read. Most didn't know I struggled as much as I did. Even if I were able to read as fast as five thousand words per minute, the rest of me still was not *new*. That would take decades.

From grade school on, I found better identity outside my own small family, which was critical and conflicted. The home of a friend in the neighborhood became a place of refuge. In time, my friend's family even included me in their vacations. I enjoyed many weekends at their summer farmhouse on a lake, only an hour from home, crewing on a small sailboat or canoeing. Significant time spent in a home that functioned 180 degrees from my own made a profound lifetime impact.

Many years of Girl Scouts taught me what I didn't learn at home, like how to get along with others. Scouting offered a wide variety of opportunities for meaningful community service to others. While camping, I learned about leadership skills, teamwork, survival skills, the value of playing, laughter, and how much fun a bunch of girls were in a tent on a rainy night. Scouting lasted into high school.

Homework was a bear, taking three to four times longer than others. Friends were honor roll students, and I managed to make the list more often than not in spite of a serious reading problem. Math made way more sense than English literature. Required book reports were a dreaded nightmare. All I knew was I was very different and not very smart. My inside was totally different from the outside.

My hiding skills carried far into adulthood, tied to self-esteem, or lack thereof. The fear that others would really know me was a solid driver to work hard, keep my head down, mouth shut, and solve the problem myself if at all possible. Beyond my fear of exposure, low self-esteem carried poor self-confidence and indecision. The pain of indecision could be both day and night.

The budding R&D organization in Denver offered the job to me. To receive this undeserved opportunity in their start-up phase as a technical recruiter utterly defied logic. Hundreds of others more qualified had competed for the job. Why me? I would have laughed hysterically four years earlier driving on ice toward Albuquerque if I learned this job would be coming on future highways! No, the whole course of events did not feel real.

All night, I lay awake completely torn by indecisive thoughts. *What if I uproot everyone, make this gigantic move to a big city where I know no one, and they realize they hired someone woefully inadequate!* As amazing as the offer was, which included a generous relocation package, as large as my fear of failure loomed, the location was the killjoy factor.

Thoughts were far from closure. *How can I uproot Hanna and Peter again? My father moved us numerous times around the country with his job, so I know firsthand the agony of a "fresh start."* Especially the move he made the summer between my junior and senior years of high school. I swore I would never do that to my children if I ever had any. But then on a deeper level, the move in my senior year was instrumental in my choice of college. And it was the year that challenged me academically to study well enough to then make it through college.

As much as I would have liked for Blake to evaporate, moving the kids away from him again could be devastating. *But wait! It could be a good thing for them also for many reasons. It's nearly impossible to parent with any consistency having a no-rules parent in town with more discretionary money and time than I have.* I had to think of the big picture, to think like a healthy parent.

The job dilemma was about more than just opportunity. A female was sorely disadvantaged competing for professional-level positions in the 70s. Women do not have the same problem today, at least not to the same extent, but few would deny the difficulty back then. As long as child support was provided on a less-than-reliable basis, my earning potential needed to be considered in a broader geographical area.

"Let's decide this together," I announced to Hanna and Peter the following day, explaining the job offer and circumstances of my current employment. In the spirit of a Ben Franklin closing, a large piece of paper was taped on the refrigerator with a vertical line drawn down the middle. On the left side at the top was written "Reasons to move to Denver." On the right side was "Reasons to stay in Albuquerque." A pen dangled on a string from a magnet between the two columns.

The company provided five days to respond. The kids and I added things to both sides as we thought of them. Typically, one thought would lead to another so we leapfrogged our way, all on board with the process, to the final day of our decision-making effort.

Both lists grew, but the left side was nearly twice the length of the right side. By day five, my eyesight resembled laser vision as I fixed my attention on the list's right side. "Leaving Daddy" was nowhere on the list. While I knew the missing words were an oversight, the glaring absence still said a great deal. I believed the Lord was in the midst of the quandary. He was providing a way that I might see His will. I accepted the offer.

I was unable to connect the critical dots at the time: (1) the pain of indecision, (2) fear and anxiety, (3) dyslexia, and (4) the fact that God loved me. Nor did I understand that *everything* big or small has a connection to God. Learning that God knew me better than I knew myself and *still loved me, a lot,* was profoundly wonderful to learn. However, moving the reality of such a supernatural wonder from my mind to my heart's operating level was blocked and overwhelmed by poor self-esteem.

The job position might even have challenged an engineer. If the job content didn't pose a problem, the sheer volume would. On average, the other recruiter and I received over one hundred résumés in a day. We recruited nationally without benefit of very many internal job descriptions, prescreened and interviewed the selected applicants, channeled the best to hiring managers. The résumés came largely from people with PhDs, some multiple. Their résumés and attached publication lists were frequently beyond my ability to understand. Some read like chemistry or physics textbooks, which wasn't totally strange because some of these people had actually written the scientific textbooks.

Brutal honesty worked best for me in recruiting when I would say, "If you cannot help me understand what you are saying in layman terms, I cannot represent you to the hiring manager." Most were quite adept at dumbing down eloquent talk and highly sophisticated bios. Often complex theories or applications were explained with drawings or simple analogies, at least to the extent needed for my work. The same technique worked internally as I became involved in the process of developing much-needed job descriptions.

Fear of failure was an incredible motivator. I kept my head down, worked at the office often without breaks and later at home from a briefcase after the kids were in bed. Work diligence led to a promotion six months later. To be out of the recruiting frenzy was like reaching the finish line in a marathon. In my frantic need to understand functions while recruiting, I had gained interest and growing knowledge in job content, how jobs fit together with others and related to compensation, organizational goals, and missions. Everything was leading to the next opportunity: to develop a job classification system, a means to evaluate hierarchical job worth, determine competitive pay.

The nature of a start-up organization is that one opportunity is followed by another. It seemed I was at the epicenter. Next, I was able to put together a means to measure and evaluate employee performance, then distribute pay increases, and bid for budgets to do so. My help came from my counterparts in other R&D organizations.

To be part of this was awesome, so far beyond anything I could ever have orchestrated. The Lord was in control—the message came through crystal clear. If He gave me something to do, He would equip me with everything I would need and more. Again, the head knowledge spun truth whether gained by experience or the Bible, but my operating level was lavishly greased and oiled with anxiety.

God was more after the fact than before, meaning I seldom prayed to seek His will. As an observer, I could see what He was doing and was quick to thank Him. Time dedicated to reading His word or praying fell off the chart of daily priorities. It was not as though I purposed to relegate Him in such a way. Getting from early morning to lights out at night was driven by time speeding at a rate that demanded full attention. I prayed when I desperately needed Him, when I came to the end of myself.

For internal help, I found a wise man with a quiet confidence and consistent availability. I knew he was busy and had a very big job, but his interest in the development of HR was genuine. He wasn't my boss or my bosses' boss. He reported directly to the executive director in a different administrative part of the organization. His employee number was three, and he often dropped into my office.

The likelihood of this person mentoring me was as remote as an eagle guiding a canary. This was the person with whom I would discuss program-development ideas. Policy and communication of everything new was a first to me, not to him. He taught me to move beyond black and white. To understand a gray area was essential if I wanted to preserve what was black and white.

Initially, we bought a house that was not as nice as our little Albuquerque home because the housing market in Denver was more costly. Still, I praised the Lord that we were able to afford something after we sold our first home. One day, driving home shortly after our move, while searching for a good music radio station, I stopped as a man was telling a funny story. While the story was great, he kept talking about the Bible.

Not at all a fan of TV evangelists or religious radio, I was surprised that the speaker held my attention all the way home. Before turning the car off, I punched the station into one of the buttons on the car radio. From then on, Charles Swindoll became a commuting companion for many years to come and the first person to disciple me in a Christian walk. I came to love the "short drive" home.

My first pay increase qualified us to move to a nicer home in a better school system. Everything looked incredibly promising—green lights and blue skies! But the traffic and weather abruptly changed without notice. Blake moved to town. In no time, the children were at the heart of ongoing conflict we left behind in Albuquerque, mostly about visitation.

"Visitation guidelines are for fathers who don't love their children as much as I do," Blake often said. "I've moved all over the country for them. How dare you to tell me when I can and cannot see them!"

Our children were repetitively put in a position requiring they make choices beyond what the divorce guidelines already spelled out. Alternating Christmases, birthdays, and holidays was supposed to happen, but almost never did. Christmas was the fiercest battle of the year. When I would cave, the accommodation became the new standard.

Whatever ground I gave was never enough. He wanted the children to live with him and often told them so. Self-employed, he could arrange time off whenever he wanted, take frequent vacations with the kids, and report income for tax purposes with his own discretion. Less time worked affected his income, so I found myself in court again when he was able to plead a case to decrease the meager child support.

"Your Honor, I'm a devoted father. I've had to move all over the country to be near my children. She's"—and he pointed to me—"a career hound."

The judge ruled in favor of the good doctor. Child support was officially cut in half, which he had already been doing on a voluntary basis for a couple of years. He found many ways to tell the children I was to blame for breaking their world apart, for breaking everyone's heart.

The topic of faith in Jesus was a frequent battleground.

"Your mother is weak and needs the crutch of religion. You don't," he explained to them. "Christianity is a huge myth, a bunch of stories. Maybe all the rules, fables, and mysteries had a place centuries ago, but science has long since disproved the beliefs, the myths. Intelligent people don't buy that fairy tale anymore. Religion is for people who can't think for themselves."

He fancied himself the supreme cultured intellect. I was pictured as the simple-minded, easily manipulated, unable to think for myself. I learned years later that on some visitation weekends, he would take Peter to humanist meetings.

"Let it go!" friends would tell me when I'd have a meltdown.

They had no clue how much I wanted to do just that! To let it go was a great cliché because the words contain a solid truth commonly applied to many things, but they might as well have advised me to try out for a linebacker position with the NFL.

These were the friends I made in the workplace. Many of us had joined the organization about the same time—the early arrivals in the burgeoning organization had developed a special comradery. They usually met Friday after work for happy hour. I would join when the kids were with their father. They were wonderful people: educated, respectable, and down-to-earth.

I listened as they offered sound counsel to one another and to me. They also valued my opinion on things. Sometimes they carried business into the casual time. Mostly, I loved the opportunity to laugh and relax in a safe group. I rarely brought up my faith in this environment. Talking about God with a drink in one hand and cigarette in the other was more than awkward. Letting go of either was not even a serious thought. Each was a source of calming the ever-present anxiety that worked better than anything else I found.

Christian friends were much fewer than other friendship circles. But their counsel regarding my ongoing difficulties with divorce no-recovery was not so different. They told me to forgive him, give it to God, and move on. They were much better Christians than I could ever have hoped to be. My thoughts about dealing with Blake were so backed up in a tangled knot of sinewy anxiety, confusion, failure, and anger that I was convinced there was no one, Christian or non-Christian, who could understand much less help me dig out of the pit of hopelessness I felt. Blake gave me new reasons, nearly daily, to deepen my pit.

However, I met a friend when I first moved to Denver who was to become unlike any other. The encounter began when I decided to attend a church party on New Year's Eve that combined single adults of three local churches. Perhaps because fewer than twenty people attended, maybe because she had red hair, or since she was tall, I noticed her and admired her.

Andrea was radiant with smiles, laughter, and kindness. She epitomized confidence and unaffected wholesomeness. She knew others at the party while I did not. Quickly, she reached out and included me. Phone numbers were exchanged between many of the guests. Andrea would later become a sister the Lord knew I craved and needed.

The whole forgiveness piece of Christianity was especially difficult for me. The drive home with Charles Swindoll was enlightening. I knew exactly *what* I needed to do; *how* to do it remained elusive. I began talking with the Lord every day, sometimes every hour about Blake. I even prayed for him. I loved the idea that he might become a Christian, and to that end, I prayed for his soul. But my prayer was selfish. I believed no Christian could behave the way he did, so my life could be instantly better if he were to come to Christ. The prayer was more about me than him, even less about Jesus.

Andrea and I got together a few times on weekends that followed. She continued to amaze me with quiet confidence and gentle spirit. She didn't have time to plan for the single-mom role she now filled. Her husband was suddenly killed on a motorcycle about two years before I met her. She was raising five children on her own.

While her circumstances were very difficult, her faith walk was real. Anyone could see that. There was plenty for which she found to thank the Lord. Before long, I valued her opinions on parenting matters more than other friends. At first, I didn't venture into the topic of divorce no-recovery, believing a widow's world was light-years different, undoubtedly more difficult than mine.

"Mom, can I have a snake?" Peter broke the silence one Saturday as the two of us drove to the grocery store. Without hesitation, I pulled off the busy four-lane road into the closest parking lot. Turning the car motor off, I swiveled to face him, intent on delivering my best-ever lecture on expectations. I was somewhat practiced at this as Hanna frequently asked for a horse. *But a snake? I'll need to soup up the regular speech big-time!*

"Are you serious, Peter?"

"Yes, Mom, they are really cool, and I've been studying them. I'd take good care of it. I've wanted one all my life."

Ten years old, all his life! *Good job, Peter!* I suppressed the laughter. But could I even imagine the first time he saw a slithery, scaly, grossly alive, and moving snake—my adorable little boy wanted to have it? To hold it? I visibly shuddered. *Deep breath!*

Every Christmas and birthday, I made herculean efforts to get them what they most wanted. Sometimes I knew what they wanted when they didn't even ask—those occasions to give were especially meaningful. But a snake! Never! So I delivered my expectation monologue, emphasizing that some desires were simply fantasies that he might have to wait until he's a man and get them himself. Peter didn't reply.

I hadn't even pulled back into traffic before I was regretting my response. *I can't believe I just did that! I utterly flattened him. Good grief! He's just a healthy, curious kid. I'm the one who has a meltdown over all things creepy-crawly, not him. Whose expectations am I cowering to? Poor kid wants to be a normal kid!*

I called my new friend Andrea. She couldn't stop laughing. She had parented cats, dogs, rabbits, rodents, all kinds of reptiles, horses, you name it; and she believed her kids were healthier as a result. She lived in the country.

"Can you tell me something about owning a lizard aquarium? My son's eleventh birthday is just around the corner. It will need an especially secure top." I spoke my request with mustered courage to the owner of a local pet store a few weeks later.

He answered my inquiry with questions about Peter. Once he learned he was a very intelligent kid with a keen interest in science, he explained, "The lizards might hold his interest for two weeks max. Beyond that, you will be left to clean a dusty aquarium." He turned me around 180 degrees to face his expert recommendation for Peter: a sixteen-inch boa constrictor.

The man could have sold Queen Elizabeth a forehead tattoo of Donald Duck. It took him ninety minutes, but ultimately, he placed Bobby Boa in my car trunk, neatly enclosed in an aquarium with climbing driftwood, a cozy warm rock, and stones for whatever snakes do with gravel. Most important was a secure locking lid.

Our next-door neighbor watched me pull into his driveway. "Hi, Ted!" I called as I waved from the driver's window. He stood next to his three-year-old while hand watering his front yard. Given zero notice, he listened raptly as I explained, "I don't have much time, my kids could bolt out the front door anytime, but I have a birthday gift for Peter in my trunk that I'm hoping you can keep until Saturday."

"Sure, what do you have in your trunk?"

"A boa constrictor." My answer might have been more carefully worded, but I was too focused on the quick mission at hand to think ahead. The poor man tried to absorb the request, but the mental lag had physical effect, robotically moving the hose nozzle toward his son. We must have resembled a sitcom. Recovery didn't take long, and he rallied to the cause. On cue, this marvelous neighbor carried the trophy aquarium gift from his house into our family room to join a lively birthday party. Once Peter grasped what the commotion was all about, he vaulted to a level of elation that didn't fade for many weeks.

The gift came with strings attached, twenty-five to be precise. Bobby's residency would change without further warnings or notice if one of the hard-and-fast twenty-five written rules were violated. At the top of the list was that Peter had to know where Bobby was always. He could not taunt anyone, shock anyone, forget to feed Bobby, blah, blah, blah. Bobby would go to college with him and on into marriage. He was expected to live thirty years. Feeding instructions were that Bobby had to have a place to eat outside his nice little aquarium habitat. We found a cardboard box. He was to dine once a week on a live mouse.

There was very little about Bobby I could even watch. Worse yet, I was leaving a barely eleven-year-old in charge of the entire operation. If I could have legally given Peter the car keys to go get the mouse, I would have done that too. Both Hanna and Peter loved the snake. Evidently, in the language of constrictors, Bobby returned affection like the pet store owner claimed he would. They were in a relationship with a snake.

When the kids were in the house, Bobby was most often clinging to one of them, hiding under a warm sweatshirt or winding his way through Hanna's long hair. Hugging either one of my children was risky, requiring precautions. Love of Bobby did not wane; it increased.

For two years, not a single violation occurred. Peter was a model snake daddy. Then just after Thanksgiving, the worst possible offense occurred—he lost him. The front doorbell rang unexpectedly one evening. Both kids lay on the family room floor with Bobby between them watching television. We all answered the door, except Bobby, and we lingered in a visit with a neighbor.

Realizing their snake was missing, Peter and Hanna quietly searched everywhere for him, terrified I would learn before they found him. They even searched inside the Kirsch curtain rods before I got home from work the next day. They removed the cloth covering on the underside of the couch, believing it was feasible he might have wound his way into the interior of the sofa. Thick as thieves, one would *never* squeal on the other. Losing Bobby was a shared problem.

Twenty-four hours passed, and they were unable to find him. They had no option remaining; they reasoned they had to tell me. Learning a boa constrictor was loose in our home ranked right up there with "the house is on fire" kind of news. Finding Bobby became the first priority for days. Sleeping in the house wasn't a problem—who could sleep? I took the next day off work and kept Peter home from school. What in the world would I have done if I found the blasted snake by myself?

"I can't put the house on the market for sale with a boa constrictor loose in it," said my realtor friend when I called her.

"Well, what if we don't specify it's a boa?"

"*Any* kind of snake," she quickly answered. "Failure to disclose the problem could result in the loss of my license, and if we disclose the problem, well, I don't really have to say anything further…" She trailed off, unable to suppress the laughter any longer that was quickly out of control. "Annie, I've been selling houses sixteen years. This is a first!"

So selling the house wasn't really an option.

Our searches were exhaustive. When one ended, I started over again. The owner of the pet store assured me that Bobby wouldn't go outside in the winter. He was still in the house. The reptile folks at the Denver Zoo told us he could live longer without food than water. Days went by. No Bobby. Weeks. One month. Two months. Three, then five. I firmly believed Bobby had exited our home through the plumbing. We eventually stopped talking about him.

While I was still trying to forgive Blake for the marriage portion of past offenses, I was confronted daily with countless new things needing forgiveness on the divorce side of marriage with him. I felt like the divorce hadn't worked. Life was so upside-down, and I was powerless to turn my world back over. I really, really wanted another divorce.

Resentment built to frustration, to anger, to infuriation, and no outlet or means to resolve from my perspective. Confronting him only yielded a more firmly planted, loathsome black hat I could not lose. With no solution, a glass of wine after work led to more than one when the kids went to bed and on weekends when they were gone. Relief was desperately needed.

My career launched like a rocket, but self-esteem lagged like a forgotten booster stage. Building skills was not tantamount to building self-esteem. In fact, the stronger I grew in the job world, the greater the contrast between the inside and outside of myself. The nastier things grew with Blake, the more intense my blaming and anger toward him. But I also turned the same intensity of loathing toward me. At some level, I believed I deserved everything he did.

Weeds in my backyard took nearly *no* water to grow, I noticed, in a drought. However, the grass required regular water, nutrients, the right balance of sun and cloudy days. I didn't plant the weeds—they arrived. Getting rid of them demanded precious time, hard work, chemicals, or maybe digging. In fact, the less water the weeds got, the *better* they grew. They always came back. Hmmmm.

The analogy with Blake was clear in my mind, but I knew I was part of the weeds. I could see bad habits took so little effort. The sin seemingly could grow with a will of its own. Sin didn't want to leave—even when I tried to ignore it, deny it, trade it, or purge it. My faith and circumstances drifted apart.

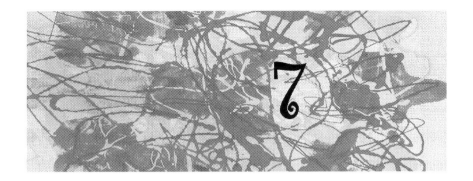

The Good Shepherd

We loved skiing together; in spite of the expense, we found a way. We would forgo a movie, or ice skating, or eating at McDonald's and throw the saved expense into the ski kitty. I would double the kitty at the end of the week. When we had enough, we would ski. We drove too far and walked too much in ski boots for a single-day trip. We planned for the best skiing experience—for more than a day with a church group to a retreat location or with other families and friends to share lodging expenses and the ski experience.

One spring break, a good friend from Wisconsin came to visit with her two daughters, Kim and Amanda, close in age to Hanna and Peter. The friendship with Heather went all the way back to days we lived in New Zealand. Our first time to ski together, we rented a condo in Vail for five days. The kids and I relished watching out-of-state people ski for the first time on Colorado snow. Many had only skied on Midwest ice. Their faces lit up like huge emoji grins, and they got good fast! Our longest ski trip ever would be the best for sure. Each day seemed to get better than the day before.

On the final night of the trip, lying in bed, I prayed.

Thank You, Lord, for the special time with the kids, with good friends, time away from the demands of work and home. Thank You for great snow conditions. Thank You for relief from the epic saga of divorce no-recovery. Thank You that I've come this far. I wouldn't be in this place without You, I fully know that. You are amazing!

The prayer led to multilayered requests. Sleep took over as prayer took me into the loving care of my Abba, Father.

Lord, I'm utterly exhausted. Physically, the ski trip has been challenging and my muscles are talking, but that's not what I'm referencing. Stretched to a breaking point on every front of my life. Honestly? Lord, I dread going back to how things are. I absolutely can't handle another single thing on my plate.

We packed the car the next morning before setting out to ski our last time, the fifth day. April 2 was an incredibly beautiful blue-sky day. Temperatures were forecast to reach sixty degrees at the base of the mountain by noon. Colorado's finest spring skiing! Successive days of skiing had taken their toll on all of us, but we knew this would be our last hurrah for the vacation and the last for the season. We found new reserves of energy and enthusiasm. Our final day would be our best!

My buddy-skiing rule came under pressure. Peter wanted to ski "black" runs with bumps. All of us had skied a few with him earlier on the trip, but we weren't game for more. By lunchtime, he pleaded for me to exempt him from the buddy rule. When he could see I was not willing to budge, he made his last-ditch effort to sway me to ski with him.

"Mom! I have the perfect last run for our trip," he said, making his most passionate plea thus far. "See here?" Peter said as he slid a trail map of the mountain across the outdoor picnic table to me. "I've figured out how we can traverse our way to the top of the highest point on that mountain by riding these different lifts. Then we ski all the way back here. There's only a small part of the whole run that's black." From the lodge at the base of the gondola, where we were eating lunch, he pointed to the highest peak on the opposite end of the mountain.

He knew what time each lift would close for the afternoon. They didn't all stop at the same time. My skiing zealot's objective to ski the longest, latest run of the day and season had a plan as well. He intended to ski like a madman until lifts started to close. Then he would work his way up the mountain lifts. At just the right time, he wanted to be the last guy off at the highest, farthest point possible as the last lift closed. The trail distance he plotted had to be three to four miles. I studied the trail map while Peter studied me.

So that's exactly what three of us did. Amanda took the bait also. We would all meet back together at the bottom of the gondola at five thirty. The lift stopped as we got off, making us the last skiers to ride to the very top that day. Glorious, stunning views awaited us, as we turned 360 degrees. Deep breaths of pure mountain air filled us with newfound clean energy. Panoramic views exploded with God's glory! Surely, we were witnessing a glimpse of heaven! Who could miss the Creator's hand?

We clustered, stamped our feet and skis, moved leg muscles as much as we could, given the rigid constraints of ski boots. Our legs needed circulation after lengthy chairlift rides.

"Ready Freddie?" we said in unison at last and pushed off the slope ledge.

We made wide, easy turns initially on comfortable intermediate slopes, using ski form I envisioned as my best ever. The terribly steep stuff would come later. Any fantasy of good form I might have would go to pot in a hurry on the bumps. For now, movement down gave no huge challenge, just uncomplicated pleasure. No other skiers came down the hill behind us, making the unique experience especially nice.

My decision at the last minute to wear jeans and a cotton blouse because of the warm spring temperatures gave added delight to the run. Some might have called me overdressed compared to a number I had seen wearing shorts and halter tops. I could feel the breeze all over my body, sensing something close to total freedom. Though the three of us skied relatively close to one another, I drifted into my own little sweet-thought world. The stillness was intoxicating, the only sound our skis carving across the top of the snow. The surrounding visuals knocked any other reality into outer space.

All serenity vaporized when Amanda fell as one of her skis broke in half. She wasn't hurt, but…what? Absolutely nothing on the run she had encountered could break a ski! Bizarre! Knowing the answer to why could not have solved the present problem—no way could she ski the distance down the mountain on one ski. We had barely started.

"Peter, you need to ski down to the mid-mountain lodge and request the snowmobile patrol to come back to carry Amanda down the mountain. Then ski the rest of the way down to the gondola and wait with Heather." Breaking my buddy-skiing rule to get help, I sent him away on the mission.

Forty-five minutes passed, but minutes felt more like hours as Amanda and I stood immobile waiting on the hill. I could only hope Peter made it safely to the lodge and then all the way down to the bottom by himself. Finally, the first sound we heard was a snowmobile coming from the distance.

Amanda and the snowmobile roared off, moving back up the hill, as I turned to face the challenges below. Leg muscles had grown cold while waiting, tight and more tired than I realized. Now in the shade side of the mountain, the cold breeze was not as welcome as it blew easily through my thin cotton blouse. Thoughts tried to stay positive as I pushed off to continue down.

Oh well, I thought, *won't take long to work up some body heat and loosen the legs.* I moved down the moderate slope, but with a different frame of mind. Spring snow, also known as corn snow, presented a different challenge to ski, especially late in the day. Catching an edge of the ski in the textured snow could happen quickly. Also, I kept reverting to a nagging thought.

Not only did I violate my buddy-skiing rule to send Peter by himself down the mountain for help, but I also violated it twice. I will ski completely alone for a very long run. In only a short distance, I came to the rim of the black-run-rated, steep, dreaded bumps that went as far down as I could see. I stopped at the edge, head spun like an owl, thoughts racing.

Nooo one is around! I've never seen a totally empty, silent ski mountain. This is eerie. Oh Peter, you said the bumps went only a short distance! Maybe on the trail map! How did I ever let you talk me into this?

Going forward would require more skill, more energy, and way more courage than I had. *Well,...son, if you can do this at your age, your mother should be able to get down this.* I pushed off with a sudden surge of newfound gusto, energy, and maybe even the tiny bit of testosterone a woman has. Unlike Peter, I didn't yell, "Geronimo!" but the takeoff was that kind of a move. *This will be the best skiing I have ever done.*

Skiing downward into the bumps, I worked my way around them successfully at first. Because of the steep hill, my speed picked up more than I wanted for the quick turns I had to make. I surprised myself and continued to negotiate my way with more control than I thought I had.

Still, speed increased. I knew my saving move at any time—just lean back into the mountain to stop. About the time I might have done just that, a ski caught an edge in the corn snow on a tight turn, crossed the other ski, and I catapulted forward totally out of control.

Finally, all motion stopped and I came to a rest. The right ski binding failed to release from the boot. The ski and boot were determined to go in opposite directions. I heard the bones crack before I even stopped moving.

I thought God reserves the worst kind of pain for the last few minutes of childbirth, right? Wrong! The damage was done—a spiral leg break, both the tibia and fibula broken in nine places. I yelled and screamed for help until I didn't have a voice. That took a while because no one heard me.

The falling air temperature and wet snow soaking into my cotton clothing ranked a distant second on a scale of discomfort. Fear took the lead as I considered the possibility that I might not be found until the next day. Most skiers know that resorts groom the slopes every night. Looking around at bumps in every direction, I recognized that bumps don't get groomed. My heart sank, and I thought I might vomit.

A lot of time passed. The excruciating pain made thinking of anything else incredibly difficult. The wonderful serenity and quietness had turned to terrifying silence. Afraid I might pass out, I talked to the Lord out loud in what was left of a pitiful voice.

Oh Lord, I know You can hear me. I am one of Yours, and I'm really in big trouble this time. I'm on top of a mountain, and You can't confuse me with anyone else. I'm the only fool up here. Last night I told you I couldn't possibly handle another thing on my plate. What a really reckless thing for me to say to You! I promise I'll never tell You again what I can handle and what I can't.

Father, this is really serious. I'm probably not going to die tonight, but at this moment, I'm not sure of anything and I'm scared to death of everything! They don't groom this slope, and I have no more voice to call attention to myself. I don't take anything for granted. You know what tomorrow holds—whether I'll be found or not. I put all my hope in You, my life…Please, Lord, I cry…Hanna and Peter don't have another mother.

Eventually, sound disturbed the silence. Big equipment started their nightly grooming on neighboring slopes. I tried calling for help again, but my puny voice could not compete with the distance or motors. Fearful thoughts increased. *Is there any way I could rescue myself? I can't move—the least little move is even more horrific! I will pass out! Maybe I could make a splint with my poles. No way! They're somewhere up the hill, out of sight, behind some huge bump.* Prayers and thoughts comingled.

I can't even think with all this pain, Lord. Pretty sure Peter reached the bottom. I pray he connects with Heather at the gondola. She will be really worried by now. I can't think with all this pain. Please keep me focused, Lord! Peter will have to show the trail map to the ski patrol. Surely, they will try to trace my path.

Would they bring Peter to help? Lord, they have so far to come to find me! It's getting so late. I can't think. It will be dark shortly. What if they can't find me—I can't yell anymore. Oh please, Lord, hear my cries! I'm soooo cold, I'm shaking all over. Is help ever coming? Even if they find me, how will I get down the mountain without moving? I can't think anymore with all this pain. Lord, I don't think I can stand this any longer ...

I heard a new sound. The source wasn't visible or very close, but definitely a different kind of mechanical noise. It didn't take long to identify the sound of a distant chairlift starting up and moving! More time passed, but the steady sound continued. More time. My ears sharpened. Soon, I heard the faint sound of skis cutting a path on snow. The Shepherd was coming: "He tends His flock like a shepherd: He gathers the lambs in His arms and carries them close to His heart; He gently leads those that have young" (Isaiah 40:11).

Strong, gentle hands and voices took over. Now, in someone else's charge, profound relief overwhelmed me. I cried and couldn't stop. Unable to articulate the feelings at the time, I knew unimaginable joy that I *would* live. I could endure whatever lay ahead. Two men with a rescue toboggan began to build a level snow platform using their skis, amid the steep bumpy terrain. All the while working, they talked to me.

Soon, two more men showed up, two who "swept" *all* ski runs at the end of the day. Soon it would be time to move me to the sled that now rested on the fabricated snow platform. But first they had to take off the ski boot on my injured leg. No words could describe the pain of the boot removal, then or now.

I'll be forever indebted to the ski patrol of Vail, Colorado. They secured the leg in a splint, wrapped me in blankets, head and all, and laid me in the sled. We started down, headfirst to counter my state of shock. I asked if any of them knew the Twenty-third Psalm. They gave a vague response and focused on their work. I asked if they wanted to say the verses with me and proceeded to recite from memory with my puny voice, not waiting for their response. Over and over I recited the familiar verses, comforted by His words, promises, and the presence of the Shepherd. I thanked the Lord repeatedly.

The unbelievably compassionate men carried the sled while skiing, instead of pulling me on the bumpy terrain while traversing the mountain trails all the way to the bottom. In doing so, the highly skilled skiers minimized additional motion-induced pain. They didn't rush, though the fading dusk worked against them.

When I arrived at the hospital after dark, even more time passed before I saw the kids and Heather. X-rays, medical records, doctors' examinations, admissions, and hospital business took priority. Finally, they let me see the kids and Heather. No words were necessary; the look on Peter's face told the whole story. We both cried as I tried to lift his awful burden.

Completely unaware of the commotion that occurred at the base of the mountain, I tried to listen to the details through the pain medications just starting to take effect. Peter had gone straight to Heather. When I didn't come down, they found authorities to tell where he last saw his mom.

My dear friend took the brunt of the other end of the storm. Finding someone who might have taken the wrong trail while skiing down a mountain at a major resort would be difficult today even with cell phones. Poor Heather frantically shuttled across the base locations of numerous chairlifts in my car with four kids, all in the dark.

Peter posed her biggest challenge. He blamed himself for talking me into the run, for leaving me to ski alone. The little man shouldered all the responsibility for the outcome, even *before* he learned the extent of my injuries. Anxious would not have adequately described him.

Heather returned to our home in Denver with everyone the next day. She had her own story of the treacherous drive through a heavy Rocky Mountain spring snowstorm that moved in the night before. I remained a guest for four days at the most expensive lodging in one of Colorado's finest ski resorts, the Vail Hospital. Sad to say, I don't remember a great deal through the fog of morphine. I do remember clearly the ninety-five-mile drive back to Denver. Blake picked me up in his van, which he had stripped to accommodate a mattress in the back. The kids rode next to me.

Mother flew up from Albuquerque to be there when I got home.

"We have an appointment tomorrow with an orthopedic surgeon who specializes in sports injuries of professional football players," my great-in-a-crisis mother announced as I came through the front door. What a joy to see my mommy! And she was in charge! If only she could make the pain go away.

"I don't want to do surgery on this leg," the well-known specialist announced his decision after reviewing X-rays the next day. "The gaps between some of these breaks are significant. If I do surgery, there's a sizable risk of staph infection. I believe the bones to be positioned well enough to fill in with calcium and heal naturally with time. Let's just leave the full leg cast they put on in Vail. Make monthly appointments to see me. The cast should come off in six months *if* the bones heal." He had the bedside manner of a power outage—no clue he just handed a single, working mom devastating news.

A rollaway bed was set up in the family room. My bedroom on the second floor of our home was virtually inaccessible for an indefinite time. Pain management at home was tough with a sorry Percocet prescription replacement for the morphine I had received for four days.

Peter appointed himself ambassador of pain relief, determined to hold my attention in what he thought would be worthy pain distractions. Games, funny stories, comic books, riddles, puppet shows, all were creative ideas that were engaging for maybe forty-five seconds. My attention span was that of a toddler in a calculus classroom. The sweet little guy never gave up or lost patience. He would just recycle his repertoire of fun ideas. It was the look on his face of love and concern that provided the needed relief and is etched in my brain forevermore.

"Sorry, honey, I have to get back to the business. You are in a lot better shape than you were four days ago. Your dad thinks he's dying all by himself," Mom said after organizing everything I would need to stay downstairs for an uncertain period of time. Friends from work showed up when she left, big-time. In fact, they swarmed us with help. They tag teamed staying overnight until I could be left alone.

My car was a stick shift, my right leg out of commission, so driving would not be possible before I was healed and out of the cast. Abby, neighbor and coworker, volunteered to supply my transportation to and from the office for the next six months once I was able to work. Maggie, another coworker, said she would do my grocery shopping for six months. Both friends achieved sainthood and never wavered. Others came in the first few days to encourage, and some brought dinner.

The children played board games on the carpet in the family room while we visited. Peter was upset the morning following one visit to discover that games were not put away with care from the night before. Little game parts were all mixed up in several different game boxes. He spread them all out on the floor and began sorting them according to the game. It didn't take long to discover Mrs. Peacock was missing from the Clue game. Hanna, along with Maggie, who was staying with us at the time, joined the thorough search of carpet throughout the family room.

"Oh, Peter, look! It's Bobby!" I cried out in drugged slow speech as I peered down the crack between my rollaway bed and the window drapery in a feeble attempt to assist searching for Mrs. Peacock. Simultaneously, Maggie, on hands and knees, had reached under the bed with her long arm and was just inches from grabbing what she thought was a scarf under the bed when I spoke.

Everything happened very fast, but my Percocet reality played the scene in slow motion, much like an animated cartoon. Maggie's body levitated up from the floor into graceful flight over the coffee table to the couch. Her entire body came to rest perched on a single toe resembling a screeching flamingo. Peter stood at the base of the bed, eyes as big as his forehead, filling with tears of pure joy at finding his long-lost boa constrictor buddy.

We would never know for certain where Bobby lived for five months, but we reasoned he had crawled into the wall behind the washer in the utility room just off the family room. What enabled his reentry into our world five months later was hard to imagine because Bobby was more dead than alive when he reappeared. Two days of water were needed before he could even eat a little. Both Hanna and Peter nursed him back to health much the way they played the central role in my recovery.

"Hey, Mom! You look like a human AK-15 assault rifle coming through that door," Peter announced to me one day as I came home from work. I moved everywhere in a wheelchair with one leg stuck straight out in front of me. The swelling in both leg and foot didn't go down for months. My toes looked like little fat purple jelly bean–shaped cars, all parked close in a row, prominently displayed as the first thing to arrive wherever I went.

When I sat in anything other than the wheelchair at home, Peter would hijack his newfound toy. "Watch this, Hanna!" He loved to impress his sister, his best friend. He learned to do amazing wheelies, lapping the circular floor plan of the house countless times, while maintaining one continuous sustained wheelie. A newborn agility led to a unicycle then overnight fame in the neighborhood, as he rode the unicycle down the block with Bobby wrapped around his head and shoulders, juggling three oranges. Yes, he learned to do that too in the produce department on boring Saturday grocery-shopping outings with Maggie.

Hanna and Peter learned to cook. We got through it. What a great testimony that the two of them were able to take an unfortunate, upending event and turn circumstances to something that worked for all of us. Certainly, an example for their mother and anyone else observing. Even eons later, the Lord revealed new insights from the episode. But the learning was always more about who the Lord is than about any of us.

He was a kind and gentle Shepherd. A tender, wonderful relationship exists between the Shepherd and His sheep. There were reasons within God's love for my broken leg, which I won't know this side of heaven. He allowed the accident to happen. I was never apart from the Shepherd, out of His sight, or beyond His reach or love. Breaking my leg was a good thing in the big picture. "And we know that God causes everything to work together for the good of those who love God and are called according to his purpose for them" (Romans 8:28, NLT). This became my life verse.

More Rope

I especially loved skiing with Andrea and her grandkids. What positively blew my mind was that she could be so upbeat and such an encouragement to others when she had been widowed only a couple of years earlier. She coped with a level of stress I could only imagine when left with five children to raise by herself. Andrea was financially lean.

Jimmy was a plumber who had not planned to leave home, much less the planet, so he left his family without provisions for the days to come in his absence. Recounting the story of Jimmy's sudden death in a motorcycle accident, she described the event from the Lord's perspective of taking him home.

The peace of Jesus in control of all things was something she lived every day and others could see was genuine. Initially, she didn't ask me about our different coping lifestyles, and I didn't volunteer information. Though we had both become Christians as adults, we were opposites in so many ways. Andrea was not a likely friend for me.

We came from totally opposite walks in life. She was part of a large closely knit family, raised in abject poverty, and country music ran in her veins. I came from an economically sound home, very small family, disconnected. Her grammar was atrocious. She was country; I was city. We dressed differently. I was preppy; she was blingy and western. I had formal education; she was self-educated. While she didn't read the self-improvement books I did, she had purposed to improve her life in countless meaningful ways that showed. The Lord had blessed her efforts. She read the Bible daily and books written by Christian authors.

I had come to live in a "corporate" world; she lived for the Lord. I was a drinker, which I did not share, and smoker, which was evident. She was neither. Different as we were, I was drawn to her, not so much because we were both single parents, but her wisdom, judgment, and remarkable faith made for a friendship experience unlike any other I had ever experienced. Time with her felt like I always came away with vastly more than I took to the relationship. Her impact was not so much with words, but more in the way she lived her life. Though two years widowed with five children, she found plenty for which to be grateful. In fact, she just didn't miss opportunities to thank the Lord. This really cut her apart from the Sunday Christian I thought I knew.

We talked easily on the ski lifts. With a scenery backdrop so rich in God's glory, even a couple of wordy women were sometimes without words. Sharing the unmistakable visibility of His presence caught us by surprise again and again. She didn't talk about others, so I knew she was not likely to talk about me. Besides, our everyday worlds were miles apart, geographically, socially, workwise, and churchwise. Our talk was about life events, parenting, our very different histories, but best of all, how we experienced the Lord, His word, and His ways. I never felt judged by Andrea. She was a safe place, so when she began asking questions on ski lifts, I began to offer up answers. The unlikely friendship grew.

We visited on the phone more than in person because of the fifty-mile drive between our homes and the sheer busyness of single-parent lives. Church, her kids, and extended family were the focal point of her life. But her friendship circles were wide, containing several deep lifetime friendships. Many times, we were invited to share some of her family events. The holidays when Hanna and Peter were with their dad did not miss her attention. Andrea and her family included me in many of them. I knew I was blessed.

She introduced me to rich Christian music concerts. Her interest in great books written by faith-based authors launched my reading of important, relevant literature. Her commitment, tenure, and volunteer work with Concerned Women of America was inspiring. Unaware at the time, Andrea was the finest mentor anyone could have, and the Lord matched us for His purposes.

Blake bought a home in our neighborhood. He took me to court for a custody change. The court ordered a social services home investigation to make the final custody recommendation. Findings: Blake was not a healthy parent. The investigator was dubious about Blake even having them for visitation. Everything might have stayed the same, but Blake increased his pressure directly on the kids to change their residency. He told them repeatedly they owed him; he had moved all over the country for them. They were over twelve years old and were legally old enough to decide for themselves which parent they preferred.

Blake promised them fun vacations, a boat, cars, parties. They wouldn't have to change schools or make their beds, clean up their rooms, or adhere to a bedtime. Conflict in our home increased as the pressure slammed sideways into adolescence. My anger was evident in *our* home. After ten years of relentless pressure, Blake persuaded Peter at the age of fourteen to see things his way during visitation for Christmas holidays. Hanna returned home; Peter did not.

The children were torn apart inside and out. The closest siblings I'd ever known, thick as thieves, a refuge to each other, loving toward each other in ways beyond their years or my understanding, were forced to choose between parents. What could be worse for a child?

God and church were in the thick of the battle. He was part of their mother's world, not their father's. The effects that Christmas would be far-reaching. Thankfully, Blake and the children did not know my struggles that ensued with God.

"Where on earth is God?" I cried several versions of the same rhetorical question into the telephone. Before Andrea could answer, I bellowed, "He's a God of love, He is good, He's just, He's in control, so *why* did He let this happen? What good could ever come of this? What did I do to cause this?" I was too busy emptying my agonizing mind and heart in a monologue to hear what she was trying to say.

Finally, she said, "I'll be there in an hour."

She listened well. Any good friend listens well, but this friend's heart was full of Jesus. Her prayers following compassionate listening turned me to hope. Hope turned my broken heart, full of hemorrhaging circumstances, in the direction of the Lord. Andrea's prayers were full of God's promises. She had packed so many into her heart from scripture that retrieving the most relevant ones for the moment was God inspired.

She was an angel of mercy. Before long, my focus changed. I began to sense the peace He promises that passes all understanding. I knew He was my hope—the only hope.

Months passed. Peter didn't know how to talk to me. He avoided. I knew all the things I shouldn't say, but what was left to talk about seemed incredibly shallow and empty given the drastic changes that had occurred. Connecting was as difficult for me as I imagined it was for him. Breaking my leg was temporary; I could endure the pain, the lengthy healing, and disruptive chaos that accompanied the process with an end in sight. Nothing about Peter's move felt temporary. The pain was an anguish that sat unmoved deep in my being. Still, I understood at an even deeper level the truth my broken leg taught me—I *can* know from His word that He will cause each and *everything* in my life to work together for my benefit, for my children's benefit, for His purposes. Though I trusted that the Lord knew everything, my heart was filled with anguish. I was the weak link for sure. This was my son, not my leg.

Lord, how can this possibly work for Peter's benefit? He's too young to understand the bigger implications of his decision. Father, he was soooo manipulated! Aren't parents supposed to be there for their children, to protect them? I failed completely.

Please have mercy, I beg You, Lord. Protect Peter from a parent who really doesn't know what he's doing. His choices and judgment are scary wrong; he serves the enemy's agenda! I know I'm dreadfully flawed, but, Lord, at least I know You and the children do too! The enemy will surely pull Peter away from You without intervention. This is not Peter's fault. It's mine! Please, Father, intervene for Peter's sake and Your good name!

And Hanna is such a hurting girl in the midst of this. Peter is not the only one. For the first time in her life, her best friend doesn't live with her. These are teen years. They are supposed to be fun, exciting, identity-discovery years, with family holding a safety net. We are so far from what our children need. Please, Lord, hold Hanna through this as only You can do!

The Lord was so faithful to deliver the peace I needed. My inability to stay focused on Him, to spend time with Him, and to *trust* Him consistently inhibited that which He longs to give every day, His lasting peace.

"Call me if you want to talk about visitation with Peter." Blake sent the message home with Hanna one Sunday night. The smirk on his face was transparent in the words Hanna relayed. Married to him was torture, but divorce from him was torture chapter two. These were extremely tough times—uncharted waters. Boiling water. Nothing provided relief from agony like alcohol. At the same time, a growing inner conflict stirred, urging caution to the budding dependency on alcohol.

I turned up my internal rhetoric that responded, *Jesus's first miracle was turning water to wine. I know some Christians who drink. I don't drink in the daytime, just after work. It's really the only thing that enables me to "let go" and relax. I don't drink near as much as Blake, nothing like my parents, and then there's my sister! I can stop anytime I want.*

"Mom! There's a policeman at the front door! He says he has a warrant for your arrest! He says you are to turn yourself in at the police station immediately!" Hanna nearly whispered into the phone, with a sizzling electric current running in her rushed tone.

Her call came in at three thirty on a Friday afternoon. Things were not even beginning to slow down at my office for the nearing weekend. We were in the throes of drafting a company-wide layoff affecting hundreds. I was sprinting as it was, knowing I needed to leave the office no later than five fifteen to meet a flight at DIA. Our friend Beverly was coming from Albuquerque for a couple of days.

"There's got to be a problem, a mistake. You sure they aren't looking for your father?" My snarky response was far from appropriate, rattling my sixteen-year-old further. Confident there was an administrative error of some kind, I asked her to assure the officer at the door that I would go to the police station immediately after work to clear things up. Convincing Hanna nothing was seriously wrong was yet another challenge. We talked for a little while, mostly about the fun things planned for the weekend with Beverly. I would pick her up as scheduled.

Climbing in the car, I transitioned my thinking to what might have gone so terribly wrong to bring about my arrest. Definitely not the way I wanted to start the long-planned weekend with an old friend coming to visit. I pulled out of the parking lot and headed to the police station, racking my brain. There was barely enough time left to stop there before racing on to the airport. Friday rush hour traffic was living up to its reputation, providing ample time to figure out there had to be a connection between the police visit Hanna received and the California stop I made a month earlier, resulting in the unpaid ticket on my desk at home. But the officer who gave it to me told me I could mail it in.

"Yes, ma'am, that's what I'm telling you," the officer said with marginal patience and practiced skill in procedure recital. "Now that you turned yourself in, you are in our custody until you can speak your case before the judge. He has gone home for the day and will not be back until Monday morning. We cannot release you."

I was powerless to do anything more than glare at Officer Bogdanovich behind the counter for a stagnate time that stood as still as I did.

"Sir, I don't mean to be disrespectful, but I got a ticket for rolling through a stop sign. It would seem I failed to pay the ticket before a deadline. I owe you $28, and I am more than happy to pay that plus a late fine, if you see appropriate. This is a terrible misunderstanding. I have my checkbook with me or credit card. I am sorry, I don't have much cash, but there is an ATM just a couple of blocks down the street at my bank, and I will go get cash if that's what's needed!"

"No, ma'am, you are now in our custody, and you are not free to leave for any reason. You'll have to work out the payment part when you talk to the judge on Monday."

"But wait! I turned myself in! Isn't that worth something? I want to pay my fine! It's a traffic violation, not a crime! People don't get arrested for an incomplete stop! I don't know how I allowed the ticket to sit in my pile of bills for more than thirty days. I meant to pay it, but I got busy and must've paid everything but the ticket. Oh, my word! This isn't happening! Please, there's got to be some mercy in all of this. Why didn't I hear from you that I was delinquent or something?"

"Ma'am, we are not a department store that will bill you when you're tardy. If you had read the back of your citation, you would've seen consequences spelled out if you failed to pay your ticket. We have a jail cell for you for the weekend. But first I have to book you. Please step around here, come with me. I need to take your photo and get your fingerprints."

It wasn't that I was being combative or uncooperative. My body would not move. I stood frozen, all dressed up in my dress-for-success navy blue suit and three-inch heels, melting down right along with the pull of gravity.

"But…" My voice cracked as vision got blurry through huge tears I couldn't hold back. "I have two teenage kids at home waiting for their mom!" I said with a pang of guilt at the half-lie—that Peter was at home with Hanna. "And I'm a single mom. And I don't have family living here to come rescue me. And I must pick up Beverly at the airport! And I'm really late! This isn't really happening, is it? Someone please wake me up." I sobbed.

"Come this way please, ma'am." He took my arm and set me in motion.

My front and side pictures taken, Officer Bogdanovich showed the first sign of mercy. "Don't worry about ever seeing these pictures, ma'am. The department doesn't have money in the budget to develop them." He rolled my fingers one by one across an ink pad as sobbing turned to ugly crying. Ceaselessly, I begged the man to let me go, to trust me that I would come back by seven Monday morning and wait an hour to see the judge at eight o'clock. I offered to leave my watch (a cheap Timex), the contents of my purse, my briefcase in the car, if he wanted collateral. I would sign anything.

"My job would be on the line if I did what you ask."

"Are you a father?" I asked in desperation that he might relate on a personal level.

"Yes, ma'am, but if I got a ticket, I would pay the ticket."

"Oh, Officer, had I read all that small print on the back of the ticket, I would've paid the ticket before I paid my mortgage." I tried to inhale. "No!" I cried. "I would've stopped fully at the blasted stop sign had I done the right thing to begin with!"

The walk to the jail cell he had in mind was silent. The heavy bars slid noisily along their tracks as he closed and locked me into a real live, wide-awake jail cell. As I watched him turn and walk away, I yelled after him in utter anguish, "Please, Officer, I beg you, wait! Don't leave me here! Please wait, *wait*! You can trust me, honest! I would be back here at seven o'clock Monday morning!"

I stood perfectly erect, motionless in shock, staring forward through the bars. No doubt I stood in the precise center of the cell, equal distance from all three walls. All my senses told me the tiny place was filthy, though I would not so much as move my head left or right to confirm. Alone, guilty, shamed, humiliated, and absolutely powerless, my head dropped back as I shifted my attention upward toward heaven.

O Lord, how I need You! I can't believe this is the first moment I thought of You. What am I doing, begging a policeman, not You? Please forgive this pitiful, messed-up me. My priorities are upside down in any way You can see them. How dare I come to You now in crisis when it seems that's really the only time I reach out to You? And what a disaster I bring—all my own making!

You know how desperately I need You and I would cry out for Your intervention, but it occurs to me that's not the prayer You want to hear most. I need to thank You for where I am, right? Not so much this dreadful place, but my gut says I'm exactly where You want me. Please, Lord! Let me hear You before I ask for anything. You know what I need most and what I would ask before a single word comes out of my mouth. You know my thoughts. While my frozen feet can't move, my heart and mind can. Please, Lord, speak to me. I'm listening.

Every muscle, vertebra, nerve, hair, and breath stood at attention. There was total silence. Time passed or stood still. I couldn't tell the difference.

Lord, I want to hear You. I need to hear You, please! I'm waiting—I can do nothing else.

More lengthy silence.

Waiting? Waiting! Am I to know somehow this relates to waiting? Muscles and nerves released just a little of their grip, but a noticeable easing. That's it! Isn't it, Lord? This is about waiting?

I took my first deep breath.

You have all my attention! I confess I've been horrible waiting for Peter to come home. I've whined to You, cried, out of anger even, expected You to do the right thing in my mind. I confess I've grown more than weary waiting for Blake to clean up his act. I totally lack patience waiting for You. In fact, I don't wait—I get in there and try to make things happen, to fix what's broken, as if I could. I know in my head what waiting for You means. Trusting You. Completely! Not telling You what to do.

The very subject of last Sunday's sermon included waiting, and I remembered the gist of a scripture the pastor unpacked: "Those who wait on the Lord will renew their strength; they will soar on wings like eagles; they will run and not be weary; and they will walk and not faint" (Isaiah 40:31, NKJV).

But my operating system has not been faithful to listen to You or wait on You. The divorce thing is just all going from bad to worse. My frenzy of frantic got me here, right? Head is light-years from heart. That should be my middle name. How long is it going to take the likes of me to get it right with You, Lord? Please forgive me. Truly, I want to get things right with You.

More silence as I shut my eyes and focused on what He had just allowed me to see. Still standing motionless, I suddenly realized waiting was two-way. God waits. The epiphany triggered more release of my body's tight grip on fear-driven thoughts. I took another deep breath and continued praying.

All the while in my self-intoxicated perspective, I've thought I've been waiting for You, Lord…You have been waiting for me! You wait patiently for me to trust You while I spiral into my frantic frenzies, again and again. You wait patiently for me to release my fears, trusting You completely with my children, with Blake. You wait patiently for me to trust Your promises that speak with such volume to me, like You will cause all things, the good, the bad, and the ugly, to work together for my good and Your purposes. You faithfully wait. When I do wait, I don't even wait patiently.

A door opened, the sound of footsteps coming near…not hurried but steadily closer. "Officer! Wha—" I said as he came to a stop standing directly in front of me.

"It could mean my job if you don't come back here early Monday morning." He abruptly slid the heavy iron door wide open.

O Lord, You are so good! Thank You for this! You have saved me from myself, but You rescued Hanna in the process! What can I say? No words are adequate—please read my heart. It is pouring out praise!

"Thank you, thank you, thank you, Officer! I give you my solemn promise, you can trust me to be back. I promise not to let you down." As I spoke, the word *promise* received my greatest emphasis, and thoughts riveted to how the Lord speaks promises to us. He never ever breaks a promise, all five thousand plus of them in the Bible. I wished the officer understood I was using the word in the strongest sense I could. My prayer hadn't ended entirely. Still, as I followed the merciful man down the hallway to precious freedom, I knew my deepest promise was shallow compared to the promises our holy Father gives us. The one flooding my mind as I walked was, "I will never leave you or forsake you" (Hebrew 13:5).

"Your Honor, I have no excuse. I should have paid the ticket when I got it. How much do I owe?" Speaking only a few feet in front of the judge at eight o'clock Monday morning, I was first on his docket.

"That will be $28."

"That's it? No fines on top of the ticket because I'm late?"

"Did you want me to fine you, ma'am?"

"Oh no, sir! I meant, well, I don't mean…well, goodness…Thank you, Your Honor."

"Next."

The layoff of nearly five hundred people went through several phases designed to carry through on the organization's mission changes. Policy makers determined that private industry would be best equipped to carry out the applications of research findings coming out of the labs. The company would focus on research. Staffing cuts were deep; administrative cuts were proportionate to technical. Many were affected whom I had had a hand in hiring. The experience was devastating for so many, but it also took a toll on those remaining.

Eventually, I received the same notification letter used to terminate all employees let go before me. The irony was I had ghostwritten the letter used by the executive director. Devastated would not describe feelings I took home late that Friday afternoon. Our little family world shook, hammered on all fronts—Blake, Peter, now my job. The job was not only our provider; work was a large part of my identity. Financially, I had limited reserves to support us during a lengthy unemployment period. Jobs were few and far between in an extremely tight job market.

Home was my place of refuge, so I couldn't get there fast enough. Not unlike many discouraging days at work or the countless days I wore the black hat in battle with Blake, I would come home, tuck my car into the garage, seek creature solaces like comfort foods and ice cream, change into pajamas, turn on mindless TV, pour a glass of wine, and engage all my best efforts to comfort myself.

I was drifting, naturally away from God. He tried to teach me in the jail cell to wait on Him, trust Him, and He would give me all the strength that was needed then and in days to come. Waiting is not just about rescue; the good Father knew what was ahead. As pain piled on top of pain, my favored method of escape, relief, and comfort became alcohol, a counterfeit comfort destined to compound agony and misery. I was in battle with "the thief who comes only to steal and kill and destroy" (John 10:10). My path was a very slippery, perilous slope.

Layoffs were going on all over the nation. The country was recovering slowly from a sizable recession; the unemployment rate had been as high as 10 percent and only just beginning to fluctuate. Finding work in an administrative field would be an arduous task, a full-time aggressive job. I reasoned that any part-time work I could find for the interim needed to be early morning or night. The *Denver Post* needed people to deliver papers. I was given a daily route of three hundred papers. My little Honda could barely hold what I picked up at 4:00 a.m., rolled, banded, and delivered before 6:00 a.m. My kids distanced themselves from me in what they emphasized was an adult route. No way were two smart teenagers going to be part of their mother's predawn insanity.

An extended employment search also allowed my participation in hospice care for my friend Abby's husband. Along with another of her good friends, a nurse, the three of us teamed up to rotate eight-hour shifts of care, extending Mitch's time at home as long as possible, about three months. The stoic retired air force colonel endured terrible cancer pain quietly. Watching him was difficult; he waived off numerous offers to see the hospice chaplain.

He and I routinely watched football games when I got to his house after church on Sunday. "Mitch, do I have permission to summarize the pastor's sermon into one hundred words or less for you? I think you would like the message." In the brief window of time before the game began, I would ask, and he always gave consent.

"Please, Mitch, I can call the hospice chaplain, and he would be here this afternoon if you would like," I offered one Sunday, his pain especially difficult.

"No," he responded, "but I'd sure like to see your pastor. Do you think he would come?"

Of course, he did! Mitch gave his life to Christ before going home to heaven.

"Mom! Do you know how many houses have your newspapers sitting on their roofs?" My slinging wrapped papers from my car window in the rainy dark, with a less-than-accurate aim onto dim porches, resulted in a real find for my teens. They might never have discovered such a "tell-on-mommy" treasure had plans not taken a turn that Thanksgiving. Hanna was spending the break with her dad and brother while I flew to Albuquerque for a much-needed three-day holiday break after Mitch passed. Talking them into my adult paper route, even for a short time in my absence, required all my HR persuasion skills and numerous promised rewards.

Denver received record snow that Thanksgiving. Twenty-three inches of snow buried the city and shut down everything, including the airport. Digging out was massive and took days. I followed the event on national news; returning to Denver was delayed. Hanna and Peter made herculean efforts to deliver the paper in my absence on the nastiest of road conditions—residential were the last to be cleared in monster storms. I didn't even ask them nor would I have asked.

Five months of full-time job searching finally landed an HR analyst position in a computer peripheral company. I was blessed to find work; many of my coworkers had not. With a tight home budget back in place, the recovery plan would take eighteen to twenty-four months to pay down credit cards and restore a little savings on a reduced income. But recovery was doable; I was employed. Another blessing—I had kept the house. Nine months into the new job with a large stable company, employment ended abruptly. The company declared bankruptcy, and my entire department was let go the same day.

Two job losses in little more than a year. Our financial situation was far from healed; we were just beginning to climb out of the hole. Another lengthy employment search would be overwhelming, and not just financially. A start-up computer peripheral company in Utah saw the opportunity to hire technical people being let go at the bankrupt company. They sent a team of technical recruiters to Denver. Technical folks were always in greater demand than administrative kinds, especially in a recession. The recruiting team had a few administrative positions to fill, which included a manager of compensation and benefits. They specifically were looking for someone to develop then manage the needed programs.

Prospects anywhere had to be considered, even moving to Utah. The offer came quickly, but I didn't respond quickly. Considering such a gigantic change felt like a no-win situation. A decision had to be made very soon. I needed work.

Hanna was in the middle of her senior year of high school. I had firsthand experience being relocated between my junior and senior year when Dad's company transferred him from Cincinnati to Utica, New York. I would lie down on a track before doing that to Hanna. Peter had moved a couple of miles away. Five hundred miles was another matter. I would never lose hope Peter would come back home.

The dilemma and options were discussed openly with the children and with a number of others I respected. Problem-solving complicity increased when Blake seized the opportunity to apply intense pressure on Hanna to change her residence immediately.

A workable option surfaced for Hanna to finish high school in Colorado and for me to accept a job offer. Hanna didn't know the Boyds well, but I did. They were wonderful people, active members of our church, rock-solid. Fran was the church secretary; Keith was a deacon and taught adult Bible studies. These honest, moral people were more than enthusiastic when I explained my circumstances and suggested they might be a part of a solution.

Experienced in family, they had parented three of their own children, now grown. Hanna's last semester of school living with the Boyds was a viable option. The plan was for me to come back at least once a month, and Hanna would come to her new home in Utah for frequent breaks/weekends.

I accepted the position tentatively, pending a search for suitable housing. The employer increased the salary offer to cover closing costs on our current home and moving expenses. Hanna and I went to Utah to search for a new home, believing her participation, though reluctant, would help in the compromises and adjustments needed ahead for her.

I bought a little VW Bug that would get her back and forth from the Boyds to the school. Financial arrangements were made with the Boyds, a much more realistic choice than another lengthy unemployment period. The benefits of living with the Boyds were enormous. They were kind, grandparent-aged, godly people, anxious to love Hanna. They already loved Hanna's mother.

I made frequent visits, attended school plays and important senior events. I prayed she would hear the Boyds' wisdom and open up to the love they had for her, and beg Blake to back off. He did not, but prayers were heard. She remained with the Boyds for the duration.

A brighter picture was ahead—following graduation. She would be coming to Utah for a full summer to visit beautiful state parks, do a little travel, and work for my employer in a summer position. There was so much to do in preparation for college when she would return to Colorado in the fall. I knew Hanna would see a bigger picture in the not-so-distant future. Not at all unlike others at the age of seventeen; she believed she knew what was best for herself. This was a time we all had to make the best of what we had. Sharing big-picture stuff with my adolescent daughter was very difficult, especially in the divided parental arena we all lived. Peter was adamant that he would remain with his dad.

To my surprise, at the end of the school year, I took a reluctant Hanna to Utah. She was resolute in her opinion that I had moved; she had not. Colorado was her home. Attending university in Colorado while I lived in Utah did nothing to rebuild the broken trust of a parent in her mind. Maturing takes time.

Jesus, Lord

S piritual counsel given to me in church and by church friends was much too noble or idealistic for my broken complicated situation. "Let go and let God" was the most frequent guidance. Such words zoomed over my head at about fifty thousand feet. They really didn't relate to my ground-level dirty epic war. True, God was in control, and this was probably the punishment I had coming for my secret dark side. No one knew I consumed as much alcohol as I did. I had become a closet alcoholic. The additional sins attendant to being a secret drinking fool were too many to count.

Relentless battles for years with my ex-husband had taken a dreadful toll. I rarely won a battle, but there was too much at stake to just not show up. Poor choice after poor choice left me consumed with resentment, anger, and all the effects of my own obsessions to dull the pain. Alcohol, avoidance, denial, blame—all earthbound options readily available and I used them, justifying any or all, given the circumstances. I lived totally in my circumstances, totally without peace in my mind or spirit. Alcohol proved more effective than any other means of coping. It also proved highly effective in separating me from my Lord.

After twelve years of single life, I began dating shortly after the move to Utah. Dating over the years had been little, sporadic, and not serious. Mostly I was incredibly busy trying to parent, work, and hold my ground with Blake. I wasn't willing to invest in a new relationship with the little discretionary time left. Truth told, I didn't trust men; and as a closet alcoholic, I knew I was a loser deal for a decent man. Well, I could see there were some good men, but they were married.

For the first time in my life, I was living alone. Living without Hanna and Peter grew old fast. Faced with a new job, living in a new state, trying to make new friends, finding a new church, I was more open to the company of others. A social circle of those hired from out of state began to gel, and we often met after work. Within the group of new friends, I met Chuck. We were both from Colorado. Friendship and respect grew, dating followed until over the course of a year; we talked of love and a future together. Hanna had finished high school and was doing well in her first year of university.

Sound reasoning told me if Chuck knew how much I drank, he wouldn't marry me; but if I didn't tell him, he'd soon learn once we married and hate me, probably leave me. His former wife was an alcoholic. He said he could spot one a mile away. In time, Chuck was worth the momentous leap to sobriety. We married for vastly different reasons.

I drank socially and never more than others in mixed company. Most friendships and social activities were work or neighborhood based, not church. Church was always present. Rarely did we miss a Sunday service, and I attended Sunday morning Bible study when Chuck would come with me. Though he professed a belief in Jesus, his walk was as worldly as mine. I sincerely intended to quit drinking entirely, quietly, the same way I sank into alcohol—unbeknownst to others. But the plan wasn't working.

Why wouldn't God help me? I pleaded with Him. A few days were all I could manage until visible shaking and mental obsessing would invariably lead to the defeating decision to postpone the effort just a little longer. Time went by. I was able to quit smoking. So many other things screamed for my attention, and I would find yet another temporary way to cope and cover up my addiction. I'd wait a while, gather my best grit, and resolve to try again, believing each time God was going to finally jump in and help. A week was the longest sobriety that ever resulted. I begged God over and over to have mercy. The efforts were gruesome. I was a closet alcoholic, and now I wanted desperately to be a closet recoveree. No one ever had to know what a dreadful thing I had been doing. No one would get hurt. I earnestly tried to stop many times but was not able.

Chuck saw me with a glass of white wine every evening after work to unwind. I bought wine by the box with a little dispensing spout and kept it in the refrigerator. It was not apparent how much was in the box, so he did not know how often I changed the box. Nor did he know the wine in my glass changed to clear vodka as soon as I found a reason to go upstairs. It was easy to refill with any one of at least twenty hidden mini vodka bottles stashed in my shoeboxes. As the evening progressed, I grew less verbal. My speech enunciation might have been a giveaway, so I grew proficient at short answers. No later evening phone calls either. Vodka has less odor than most other drinks and was the chosen drink for that very reason.

Perhaps the biggest deceit was when I walked through the front door every evening; I had already consumed two minibottles of vodka on the way home. These I picked up at drive-through liquor stores en route to home and poured the contents into my empty coffee cup in the console of the car. Each minibottle contained two ounces.

To get community-based substance abuse help carried huge risk—way too much at stake to lose! The fear of discovery was nearly paralyzing. The city I lived in was not that big—HR people were too well connected. I would be the juiciest subject of gossip in no time at all, unemployed at that. Many conversations with God went something like

> *Lord, Chuck will leave for sure. I've lived such a horrible lie right under his nose! The lie has been in place for the entire two and a half years of our marriage. If I don't beat this, my Christian testimony will be ruined! What an* incredible

hypocrite I am! Oh, Father, how did things get this bad? What on earth will my children think? Friends? What would become of them? Especially Andrea, she'd never respect me again. The church? Oh, I can't even imagine! This would definitely be the last nail Blake would need to drive into my coffin. What irony is that? He's been the alcoholic since before I even left him! No question, I'd lose my children's respect, my job, my career destroyed!

I created this horrendous problem—it looks like You expect me to dig out alone. How could I blame You? I've totally mocked the gift of salvation You freely gave to me. Oh Jesus, I threw You under the bus to cope with pain and now I look like the rest of the world, only worse! Can You ever forgive me? I've tried, really tried and cannot do this by myself. It isn't just about me—my horrific choices, if known, will hurt so many others. I'm begging for another chance to be a decent, honest Christian. I'm so scared, so over my head, every day I sink to a new low!

By now, I was an HR manager tasked with identifying possible chemical dependency in the workforce. Periodically, I would pore over attendance records of 1,200 people, looking for absentee patterns around weekends and holidays. What a despicable person I had become! I utterly hated those days in my job, but made certain my absences didn't fit the telltale pattern.

Each failed attempt to quit drinking took more and more out of me. I loathed myself more and more. I had been a hypocrite before I married Chuck, but now I reached new levels in carnal Christianity that would rival a KKK member. My secret inside person was nothing like the outside. Being a *functional alcoholic* contributed to all the factors allowing me to carry on the crafted facade, undetected by others, for such a sustained period of time. In retrospect it was clear that my conscience knew right from wrong—the tension created by a speaking conscience steadily grew stronger until it was intolerable.

I literally ached inside. Alcohol was so much bigger than the Lord in my life. I knew I was detestable to the Lord.

Chuck was still sleeping next to me. My eyes were wide open, trying to ignore the pounding of another stinking headache that was present every single morning. Thoughts that haunted me every minute of the day had invaded the nights as well. Sleep was nearly as miserable as being awake. Just getting out of bed seemed to take more strength than I could muster.

But this Saturday morning was not going to be a pathetic rerun. I *knew* this day was going to be different. A growing sense that everything dark inside me was going to spill out shortly had my total attention. The dreadful long-held secrets were about to be no more. Not one more day! I'd rather die than live another day with another lie. Whatever the consequences, they could not be as unbearable as the abysmal life I was leading. A volcano of molten confessional ash was about to spew. I closed my eyes, accepting whatever was coming. Lying motionless for several minutes, hot tears welled up as I began to pray.

O Lord, I didn't even know what grace was before I met You. You have showered me with Your holy mercies when I really should be dead for all the evil in my life. I'm going to need that kind of deep mercy to wipe away my sins surrounding alcohol. The lying, the selfishness, the arrogance! Not just alcohol. You have never really been the Lord of my life. My own strong will, driven by fear, has sought all my own comforts, my ways, not Yours. What a fool I am! In my brokenness, I've responded in my own strength when I could have had Yours. How detestable my ways are to You!

You are a very, very big God and so is my ask because I know just how seriously bad I've been. First, I've sinned against You, then my children, then my family and good friends. This has gone on for way too long, but You know every bit about my dirty secrets. Whatever You decide to do with me is more grace than I deserve. Justice would be to end my life, so anything less is mercy. I just want to be truthful with You before I see You face-to-face and honest with everyone else. I beg You, clean me up from the inside out and give me a fresh, clean, new spirit. I pray You will restore the joy of my salvation. I seek Your righteousness. I have nothing to offer but a broken remorseful spirit.

Thoughts flooded my mind of my salvation experience on Easter Sunday thirteen years previously. How precious the memory of Jesus calling me as He told me the story of Peter boldly stepping out of his fishing boat. Wonderful thoughts I would always guard as some of the very best in my life—right up there with the birth of my children! "'Come!' Jesus said. Then Peter got down out of the boat, walked on the water and came toward Jesus" (Matthew 14:29).

An avalanche of blessings He poured out on us right after my confession of belief! And so many more followed. But oh, how far I had traveled in the wrong direction since that day, through one storm after another! Compounding one sin on top of another to construct such a sorry double life! Nothing I was doing could possibly be a blessing to Jesus.

Then memories of Peter on the water continued. But when Peter momentarily moved his focus from Jesus to the powerful wind, he became afraid and started to sink into the water. Peter cried out, "Lord, save me!" Immediately, Jesus reached out His hand and caught him. "You of little faith," He said, "why did you doubt?" (Matthew 14:30–31).

It is true, Jesus! I am sinking in my circumstances because that's where I totally live, doing my utmost to control everything but controlling absolutely nothing! It is entirely true that I don't have my eyes on You. They dart everywhere else just like my chaotic dyslexia at its worst. It is also true I live in a perpetual state of worry and anxiety, fearing I will be overcome and discovered at any minute. It is true I am a drowning nasty carnal Christian. Can You ever forgive me, Lord Jesus? I have no place asking You to rescue me—You did that already, and I didn't deserve it the first time. Still, I have nowhere else to turn. I have only You. Please, Lord Jesus, I beg You to give me a second chance, please save me from myself!

I just knew the Lord had me by the hand and was taking me into the Light, out of the storm. Whatever was to come, He assured me He would take me through—sober. I *wanted* to go with Him, wherever He went. My choice, my free will, was being exercised. It was *the* moment of surrender. Jesus became Lord of my life, not just my Savior on that Saturday morning. He pulled me out of my stormy circumstances and into His arms. The day began in a milestone moment of total honesty, repentance and surrender, trust in Jesus.

The act of surrender was an act of flat-out trust. For me, it had nothing to do with my mind/head but all to do with my heart and spirit. As I took His hand, I was released from the tyranny of anxiety, fear, *all* sin. The volcano I expected to spew molten lava was doused, sewn shut, or sucked back deep in the earth. I have no idea what became of it, but now I saw a sleeping Chuck in a totally different way. I knew I had to tell him everything if all the deceit were to stop. He was so peaceful, oblivious that his easygoing world was about to turn upside down. My concern was for the man who trusted me but would learn shortly the full extent of my actions that wholly violated his trust, mocked our marriage. I prayed the love we shared in Christ would cover the collateral damage I had done to him.

Chuck's image of me was a rock of stability. In his mind, he married a woman who had a great job, owned a house, lived a life outwardly steeped in ethics, valued all the right things, and was as reliable as a Seiko watch. His life was in a season of utter chaos when we met, so our marriage had marked a welcome turning point for him.

Telling Chuck that I was a closet alcoholic who consumed eight to ten ounces of alcohol after 5:00 p.m. *daily* since before we got married turned out to be more problematic than actually quitting the addiction. I effectively pulled the rug out from under him. At first, he didn't even believe what he heard. Why would he? We had been married for two and a half years, and he was clueless that I had lived a different life than he shared with me. I might as well have told him I had another husband squirrelled away he didn't know about. I deceived him beyond forgiveness. He was not the picture of support. God was.

"I'm out of this charade we've called marriage!" His fury fueled the most-dreaded response, volume rising rapidly along with threats of widespread communication. He would expose his phony wife to everyone who thought she was somebody. Whatever I thought I might have offered in terms of apology or explanation vaporized. I was silent while he raged, save the repetitive barely audible "I'm so sorry." He had been betrayed and was fully justified. No doubt he would have carried through with his angry intentions, but constraints caused him to hesitate.

His troubled adolescent son had come to live with us shortly after we married. Over the span of just two years, the teen had surrendered his life to Christ and was well on his way to being a great joy to both of us. He was sold out, having found genuine freedom in a truth and intimacy in Christ he never knew. He was focused in school for the first time, achieving grades he had never seen. A dramatically changed youth, he was active in church and even leading other youth to the Lord. His amazing new life amazed his dad more than anyone. While Chuck couldn't have been prouder of the changed life we witnessed, he was baffled. Looking back, his son had something he didn't have—an uncomplicated intimacy with Jesus, but Chuck could not have articulated the difference. What he did understand was to uproot the boy would be damaging to say the least. Second, Chuck was between jobs with no income.

Moving ahead on a rocky road of recovery with a reluctant, angry, distrusting partner would seem to be a formula for certain failure. For six weeks, Chuck pouted and avoided. I found solace going to work. The Lord's comfort and encouragement came from unexpected places. Early one morning driving to the office during the first week of my brand-new sobriety journey, Amy Grant was on my car radio, singing a song that became my mantra for the first few awkward weeks then months. She sang "I Have Decided."

> I have decided,
> I'm gonna live like a believer,
> Turn my back on the deceiver,
> I'm gonna live what I believe.
> I have decided,
> Being good is just a fable,
> I just can't 'cause I'm not able.
> I'm gonna leave it to the Lord.
> (Songwriter, Michael Card)

If I needed a bridge to lock hands with Jesus, "I Have Decided" filled the need. I bought the tape, and it stayed in the tape player of the car. Amy sang the words of truth that only the Lord could do what I wasn't able to do. I needed the encouragement en route to work and back. The Lord used the music to expose the lie I had lived and the blessed hope of change in Him. She sang when I ran errands. Sometimes at ten thirty at night in my pajamas and robe, I'd crawl into the car to hear the words again before I could sleep. My decision to trust Jesus as Lord meant I was finished living a lie, enslaved in sin. Eventually, she sang in my head whenever I needed her.

I thanked God all day long, talked everything over with Him, just couldn't wait to hear from Jesus, and He faithfully communicated with me. His Word spoke timely power messages to me, prepared long before their delivery, in Sunday morning sermons, or as a Bible verse hanging near a coworker's computer, messages about Jesus's love scrawled in the dirt of a car's rear window, a phone call from Andrea, or even a billboard on the highway. He showed Himself to be unlimited and wireless in communication. He knew I needed to simply stay focused on Him. The rest of my life was radically changing. "Try harder" was gone; I was in His company. No shakes, no panics, zero regrets, no tears, and no fears.

I was keenly aware that the changes occurring were not just a euphoric flash in the pan. I could not look beyond today—at the same time, I knew if the Lord was more than enough for today, He would be more than enough for tomorrow, one day at a time; no two look alike. My confidence was not in me; it was in Him. There was no safer place to be. I prayed for Chuck, for his son, for my children in Colorado, for all our needs—a job for Chuck. I prayed for our devoted pastor—suddenly, his Sunday messages were sinking in deep. The changes occurring in me were not isolated; all who walk through the doors of a church are sinners seeking to know Him.

Six weeks sober marked a milestone in many ways. Chuck and I didn't discuss drinking until I brought it up at the six-week mark. Though we hadn't spoken of the elephant in the room, Chuck watched it like a hawk.

"To talk about it is too soon for me," he mocked me, accusing me of even implying I might be cured in a few brief weeks. "I seriously doubt you will be able to quit."

"The Lord meant me to be accountable to you, or I could have quit without your ever knowing," I explained my reasoning for finally vocalizing. "Believe me, this is the Lord's way, not mine. Hurting you was the last thing I wanted to do."

"So you think the Lord wanted to hurt *me*?" Chuck spoke a bitter response, showing hurt for the first time in his eyes, not so much anger.

"I can only imagine how much I've hurt you. There are so many things about what I've done that were wrong." I began talking about the hypocrisy and unspeakable shame of even attending church while I hid my secret.

"My children have been deceived the longest. I really, really, really hope I'll never have to tell them."

"What makes you think they don't already know?"

"If they must know, I pray the Lord will allow me to be the one to tell them at the right time," I continued expressing my regrets. "What a hypocrite I have been to counsel employees to seek help when a drinking problem affects their work performance." I unloaded countless ways my alcoholic lifestyle had resulted in other sin. Pure and simple sin. Loads of confession. Chuck listened.

"I was a fool to think if you never knew my secret, I wouldn't hurt you. I honestly believed I could quietly quit without having to tell anyone, you especially. Outrageously lame thinking! But my secret was way more than just alcohol. To keep alcohol dependency secret for nearly six years required thousands of lies. First were the lies I told myself. Then lies I told the Lord, like I could deceive Him. The lies of omission and outright untruths I told you, my kids, every friend, and my family. I was so incredibly selfish in it all. A loving and long-faithful Father intervened, and I'll praise Him to my dying day for doing so. Still, I have been such a lowlife that you have been serious collateral damage because of what I have done.

"Chuck, I should be dead. Why the Lord let me live to this point is really the question. He is long-suffering, and the likes of me is the reason why! Really, how can anything good come from a life like mine? I'm worse than the worst Pharisee—they're the only ones who really made Jesus mad." Chuck listened as I inadvertently talked my way down a self-condemning path, initiating thoughts of fear and fading confidence.

"The Bible is full of second-chance people," Chuck offered, observing how my expression and words had betrayed my underlying feelings.

I stared at him in disbelief. His words opened a sorely needed relationship door, spiritual-insight doors, and great hope. "I begged God for a second chance, Chuck. I didn't tell you that." I spoke tearfully and remembered simultaneously. "I used those very words."

We were engaged in heavy conversation—Chuck's listening was as intense as my efforts to convey things I was just coming to understand. However, our demeanors were not the same. I could see I still had not answered his first question.

"Chuck, I'm not able to answer your question directly, whether the Lord meant to hurt you. He does nothing that is not in love—that is solid truth. But what He does doesn't always look like love to us. Our character is much more important to Him than our comfort. He's our Father, disciplining, teaching, refining, and rewarding us continually to conform us in love to the image of Christ. The Bible speaks quite a lot to suffering and experiencing pain. While it doesn't fully explain why we suffer, we can trust Him that it serves His greater purposes. Jesus told us to expect trouble in this world."

"That's kind of brutal when you put it that way."

"His Word also says to take heart because He has overcome the world. His Word speaks at length of joy, satisfaction, rewards, and tons of things we welcome that He also gives in love. I just know the two sides of all this are woven together by the hand of God. He is wise, light-years beyond our understanding. There's no way we'll completely see or appreciate Him this side of heaven. We see only a little—enough to know it's Him, want to know Him more, and trust Him.

"He knows what He's doing, Chuck. We don't. I'm only speaking of God's ways in *this* problem, in my own life. Even then, I won't ever fully understand them. I love that He has shown me some of His ways. If *you* ask Him the same question and trust, He will answer your question. It's all about being right with God. I trust Him when He says He will cause *everything* to work together for our good and for His purpose. I learned that on the side of a mountain.

"He's working in your life as surely as He's working in mine. He is sovereign, in control. Well, I just pulled my own thinking out of the ditch. Though I can't see ahead, He will make something good of the dark side of my life, now that it's in the light. I *know* He will. He's already begun.

"I suspect regaining your trust or respect will take a while. I cannot even ask you to give me that much, but I *can* ask the Lord to speak His will to you. I can pray that your heart and mind will be open to what He has to say to you, that He will help you to forgive me. We've *both* been on an extremely difficult journey these past few weeks. It might not be quite so difficult if we traveled it together. We might even start by praying together.

When I told him I needed him in a practical way starting now, he was skeptical.

"Oh, it's easy. When I say 'Wow, I could sure use a drink,' just come alongside and put your arm around my shoulders. Then please say, 'It's okay, honey, you've already had yours.'" We both laughed until we finally cried. We prayed. I got my first hug.

Trying to use the support model infrequently but when really needed took time. Eventually, Chuck even sounded sincere and supportive. His support was needed, much appreciated.

Even more profound than the alcohol recovery was the emergence of a new me, much like the teenage days when learning to read freed me from some dyslexia limitations and left me incredibly exhilarated. But those feelings were multiplied a thousand times. This was not just a feeling; I *knew* that an inside-out, down-to-my-cell-level change was happening. I trusted the Lord like never before. I was free from the lies and secrets, free of the bondage of addiction, free of the continual self-debasing. To be authentic, honest to the bone, free to grow as a child of the King, was the soil needed to begin meaningful faith walking.

I was free of the sin that had separated me from the Lord. I celebrated each new day of sobriety with Jesus. No one else but Jesus held my hand nor were they needed as it all turned out. Jesus was my GPS. Inside, I was a cracker box of exploding praise, insights, and confidence in the Lord. It showed on the outside. People asked me what changed. They reported seeing a new kind of confidence and demeanor. While I considered it wise to be unspecific about my victory, I seized the opportunity to share excitement in a faithful, merciful, loving, and trustworthy God.

The level of trust I was finding opened a whole new world. It took me thirteen years to put wheels on my faith. I discovered faith is a narrative. Mine stalled in infancy until I decided to be honest. I sang my victory.

If We're Honest
Truth is harder than a lie.
The dark seems safer than the light.
And everyone has a heart that loves to hide.
I'm a mess and so are you.

Don't pretend to be something that you're not.
Living life afraid of getting caught.
There is freedom found when we lay our secrets down at
the cross, at the cross.
If we're honest.
(Francesca Battistelli)

The Terrorist Within

We returned to Colorado, bought a house, joined a great church, got jobs, and jumped into the years that were about to fly by. Both Hanna and Peter completed bachelor's degrees in the sciences. What a joy to go to their graduations! Peter married a very sweet young Christian woman a couple of years after school. She was third generation in her church, and it was picture-perfect to see them married there. He pursued work in environmental science then transitioned into information technology while Hanna continued in school to receive a master's degree to teach math and science in middle school.

My children were such an inspiration to me that I also returned to school. It seemed appropriate to get a master's degree in the field in which I had worked for twenty years. Hanna and Peter remained best friends, although my heart grew concerned as I observed both drifting farther and farther from the Lord.

Fatherhood suited Peter like teaching suited Hanna. His firstborn were twins, a boy and a girl, followed by another boy two years later who quickly became a "wannabe twin." All three were inseparable friends, much like Hanna and Peter were from an early age. Hanna excelled in teaching, winning excellence awards in the state's largest county. Her teaching inspired students to pursue careers in science.

Peter excelled in family in every way. His children were raised without a television in the home, knowing from an early age that learning was exciting, playing as a family the absolute best. While not untouched by the unending divorce, they were both remarkably strong in moral character, which served them well. I prayed continually for their return to worship of the Lord.

Trusting me as Chuck once had would never return entirely. His walk with Jesus was different from mine. He was not inclined to share his faith with others, especially me. I quietly questioned the intimacy of his personal relationship with Jesus. We struggled in the marriage. Our temperaments were opposite, so were our priorities.

Chuck had difficulty holding a job more than a couple of years. As smart as he was, relational issues were difficult for him and proved to be an employment inhibitor. We began looking for a franchise business to purchase that could make better use of his skills. After searching a few years, we purchased a license to open a cleaning business of commercial facilities with an excellent national reputation. By this time, I was working as an HR manager for an IT consulting firm and teaching at a local university in the evenings. I loved opportunities to participate with some technical teams in change management with customers transitioning in mergers. I was absolutely loving my working life!

Both of us were required to attend a two-week new-owner training and orientation at the corporate home office. Once completed, we were advised that Chuck should continue working in his current job to provide a revenue stream, and I was more ideal to launch the business because of my HR background. When the business could support both of us, I would return to my profession. The counsel we received would turn my world upside down.

"Ma'am, Mr. Brown is very busy and won't be able to see you. Why don't you leave your card and he will call you?"

"Oh, I'll wait, no problem." My first sales approach was about to pay off and become my model for many more to come.

"But, ma'am, that could be quite a while."

I would smile and assure the receptionist that I had the time and didn't mind waiting. While I sat patiently in their waiting room, I would take in the surroundings with a critical eye, maybe ask to use a restroom. My purpose was to find dirt, anything the current cleaning company may have missed. After a little while, the receptionist was motivated to see me disappear. She would let Mr. Manager know I was waiting. If I were there for very long, she might remind the manager. Eventually, Mr. Manager would emerge from somewhere in the back, perhaps even irritated by my prolonged presence. I'd introduce myself, chat just a little, and quickly get to my purpose.

"While I was sitting in your reception area, which is your first impression to all new clients or customers, I couldn't help but notice windows that need cleaning, or a cobweb in the entry, or soil on the upholstered chairs or carpet. I'm not sure who your cleaning service provider is or what you pay, but I would love to talk with you about a service I can offer so that guests could not find what I have been able to see." My investment of time was nearly always rewarded with a meeting. If not, then at least an appointment. I was not a salesperson, but if I could get the first appointment, my HR experience in manufacturing environments allowed me to relate on topics of common interest and approach a potential customer with a little credibility.

The Lord blessed the business, growing it rapidly. Selling in the daytime, cleaning at night. I had to hire others when I started changing selling clothes to cleaning clothes in the car. The training we were initially given provided business operating models that I followed to the letter. Knowledge plus experience led to more growth. The customers we had were a wide variety of businesses, ranging from manufacturing, a chain of day care centers, dialysis centers, banks, general office buildings, and so on. A year and a half into a whole new world, I told friends I was beginning to feel like

Forrest Gump. Where would the Lord lead next? No amount of imagination would have answered that question.

While my small family in Albuquerque was not very connected, I was finding that Dad had given me a great deal growing up that I needed to go forward when I left Blake. He was the giant in my life. The gold standard. It wasn't like he was the ideal father; he wasn't. But he was *my* father. His job was everything to him so I knew it had to be a very important job to need the likes of my father.

Although not a religious man, he was one of the most moral people I knew. He could always be counted on to do the right thing. Even when it was hard. When it cost him money or time. Even when it cost him face. I had a moral compass that pointed me to God when my father was no longer the authority in my life, or my rescuer, or my provider. The trust I had for my Heavenly Father began with my earthly father. Integrity was his defining character trait.

To the extent that I was able to write with some technical help and participate in evaluating the relative worth of hundreds of job descriptions from R&D work environments, computer technology-based companies, and mining engineering, I would credit my father. Often after dinner, he would pull his pen from his pocket and begin drawing on his napkin as he answered my questions about how radios worked, or what made airplanes fly, or why we could get power from dammed-up water. Later, I would not be able to explain a concept without a dry eraser and whiteboard or pencil and paper. I quickly grasped concepts explained in technical jobs.

Dad was left-brained, and I was right-brained, which probably accounted for many of our differences. He was a man that if you asked him how he really felt about something, you wouldn't get words back, just an annoyed stare. We were never close, but our relationship changed in his advanced years. As his left brain began to let him down, his body moved more brain function to the right side. He let me in.

Memories of a Thanksgiving in the hospital with Dad in his last years were especially tender. Just the two of us. Dad was in nasty pain. Following leg surgery, his long incision was left open to combat staph infection and provide access for frequent painful cleanings. I took Mom's food from the feast she prepared, along with plates, silver, and even candles, to the hospital to make his day something better than the day before. That memorable day, he allowed me to pray with him for the first time. And the next. And on each subsequent visit made to Albuquerque for his increasing hospitalizations. We often spoke of the Lord. My fervent prayer was he would come back to the Lord he knew growing up in Raleigh, North Carolina. At the same time Dad was beginning to struggle with health issues, our cleaning business was budding.

One summer day, I received a call from the regional marketing manager of our parent corporation, asking if he could come to our home that evening. He had something to discuss with us.

"You don't suppose he wants to sell us Amway?" I said to Chuck in nervous half humor as we speculated about the coming guest. Allen was an easy communicator. We knew him from church as well as business. We all ate a piece of pie and enjoyed catch-up conversation. He was kind to inquire about my father and offer prayer.

"Your business growth has been of interest at the national level." Allen got to the business point. "We know many franchises are bought to provide a job for the owner, but your business shot up like a textbook template they have been following."

"Oh wow, Allen! I wasn't expecting this. Honestly, I think I've just been in a hurry to reach a size where Chuck gets the operation and I can get back to my HR world. The Lord has been very generous." I could feel the pride monster rise and struggled to at least sound humble. I certainly wasn't willing to tell him that providing a job for Chuck was the very logic in purchasing the franchise.

"What I want to discuss is an opportunity that has come to

national we think you might be ideal to take on. There are other larger franchises in the region and older ones, but *how* you have begun yours might make you a good candidate for this opportunity. How would you like to clean the Broncos stadium?"

"What part of it?" Finally able to speak, breathing and talking were supposed to happen together. I struggled to do either.

"All of it. The whole thing. Seventy-six thousand seats, concourses, locker rooms, the boxes, parking lots. Snow removal. You have three days following a game to get it all clean. The first preseason game is August 8."

"In three weeks?" Speaking wasn't getting easier; I spoke an octave higher as fast as diction would come out. "Oh, Allen! How on earth do you even bid something like that? Will national help?" Thoughts were chaotic and strange. *Football is not my thing. Do they know I don't even know what a first down is?*

"There's a franchise in New York that has done five cleanups in their NFL stadium. I know the guy, and I'm pretty sure he would help you with a bid, even though the stadiums are very different and he's only just started himself. At least it's a place to begin. Give him a call, Annie."

"Call? I'll send him an airline ticket to come out here and help. Yes, of course, if the Lord is leading, we want this. He'll provide the way and equip us." My expressed trust was far from the anxiety I felt inside—like I had instant carbonated blood. "Allen, I cannot believe you had enough confidence in us to even consider us. How can I possibly say thank you?"

"I prayed about it. You can thank the Lord." Allen smiled like a big yellow emoji.

"Yes, and we need to do the same." I glanced at Chuck who was grinning even bigger than Allen.

As he left, I prayed the Lord would forgive me for my lagging trust in Him that I had not honestly expressed to Allen only minutes earlier. My fear level was over the top even though my gut told me the Lord was leading. Nothing was ever ordinary where He led.

Cleaning up after a football game would take practice, but we didn't have time. My colleague in New York City helped me assemble a bid for a contract, but a pretty colorful notebook with best-guess costs was as distant from the actual cleaning job as kindergarten would be from high school graduation. If I thought the Lord blessed the business for the first year and a half, the blessings had barely begun. A rocket of blessings launched three weeks later when we cleaned the stadium after the Broncos' first pre-season game.

Miguel was a secret weapon I was convinced the Lord provided. He spoke a little English, which was a great deal more than the rest of the people I hired. Miguel had zero experience in professional cleaning and, of course, none in stadium cleaning. He had lost his job of ten years in the garment industry because the small business owner's brother needed a job. Wanting to work was my only job requirement. Speaking a little English and wanting badly to work made the man my star employee on the third day of the brand-new stadium contract. By the fifth day, I promoted him to supervisor. Many of the employees we hired had worked for the former company. Miguel was instructed to tell them a different work ethic would be required.

My limited Spanish began eons earlier in high school, but I quickly learned "cleaning Spanish." Because I used the little I knew and would work alongside them at times, my efforts went a long way to bridge cultural gaps. Relationships began. Miguel was a natural leader, kind, patient, and respectful. He demonstrated the work ethic needed, learning all the many operations used to clean up after a football game. Shortly, we needed at least two levels of supervision. Employees highly respected Miguel. We built on the right stuff. While the Broncos scored touchdowns, we knocked the first game out of the park. And the second. And the third.

My human resources career was born out of desperation, not education or experience, but the Lord himself led and enabled the entire twenty-three years step by step. The event center cleaning was born out of thin air and took an amazing shape nearly overnight. One morning, I received a phone call from the manager of the Denver Coliseum and Red Rocks Amphitheater.

"I'm impressed with what I'm hearing," Mr. Barns said, "that you guys are hauling dirt out of the stadium that has been there fifty years. I would like you to bid the contract I am about to open to bidders."

"I thank you very much and couldn't be more flattered but, Mr. Barns, I do not even meet your minimum qualifications to bid. I have only been doing this a year."

"Lady, if you can clean that place the way I'm hearing, you'll have no problem with my facilities. I make the decisions around here so don't you worry about the paper part."

We bid. We got it. No one could believe what we were doing, least of all me. My days were surreal because I was faith-living, step by step, in uncharted territory. Praising the Lord and breathing were as natural as inhaling and exhaling, and they happened together. We added the Bandimere Speedway and soon found a pace we could handle.

When news reached us that a new Broncos stadium would be built immediately adjacent to the current one, I knew we would be the best contender for a contract if we could do the construction cleanup. We bid it. We got it, 1.8 million square feet, plus all the glass, signage, all of it to be cleaned in two months. We partnered the effort with another small business that specialized in construction cleanup. They had more specialized cleanup expertise; we had more workforce. Cleanup went well, but the coming bombshell brewing behind walls was beyond my ability to see, much less anticipate.

My competition was big business—the real deal. They bid the

contract for the new stadium too, to include food in addition to cleaning, and won the contract. We lost.

Meanwhile, Chuck's working world for his computer peripheral employer was changing. His value was discovered coordinating the importation of needed component products from Germany. As a result, Chuck's job continued longer than expected. Career lust consumed him with frequent business trips to Europe nearly monthly. He quickly racked up frequent flyer miles, flew first-class, stayed in five-star hotels. The commercial cleaning business was never meant to be just mine, but despite rapid growth or demands, cleaning up after others no longer appealed to Chuck. He had finally found his career choice. And not so much appeal for marriage either.

He eventually turned all the pent-up anger he had long held toward others, his worst dark side, toward me. He slammed doors repeatedly until plaster around the doorjamb crumbled to the floor. He found European women, a new world, a new continent, a new life. When Chuck left, he broke my heart. He shattered me along with the doorjambs and discarded fallen plaster.

Timing was brutal. Chuck left the marriage. Not a whole week after, I learned we lost the stadium bid. Then a week later, Dad died. So in less than two weeks, in late August of 2001, my world imploded. My two towers came down just weeks before terrorists took down the World Trade Center.

My prayers were as fractured as my life. While I didn't doubt the Lord was in the midst of it all, I could not feel Him. Darkness was what I felt. Questions of God didn't feel holy or reverent. I thought they were best kept inside. Just taking one step after another took utter focused concentration. Beneath the thin facade, heartache consumed all my senses, mind, and body. As I headed home from Albuquerque, totally numb after Dad's death, the drive became the prayer most needed and the release of honest feelings. The compassionate Lord leaned close and pulled prayers out of me. I cried out my broken, knotted, seriously wounded heart to the Lord for 450 miles. There is no finer Listener, and eventually I was able to listen to Him.

Oh, Father! This is scary awful! I have no control. I just want to curl up in a ball and roll away, far away, forever! Why can't I feel you? You have never left me or failed me. You have been faithful when I have not. There's nothing outside Your sovereign reign. Why do I feel like I am? Please don't let me lose my mind! You are here, right?

Please, have mercy, Jesus! This is torture not knowing where Dad is. Please give me peace about my father! Is he with You? One more time, just one more, I needed to make certain he was coming to You! I thought I was doing Your will when I was with him. I wasn't finished! Why did You take him so soon? I miss him so, so, so bad; we were just starting to know each other. What must Mom be going through? Lord, be with her! She doesn't even know You, but You know her! Protect her and please give her comfort! Why isn't Chuck here? Of all times, I desperately need my husband! I cannot do this alone, Father! I can't lose them both! They are my twin towers!

This is so unfair! Was I not doing Your will with Dad? Have I not stayed in this marriage for the primary reason to honor You in my promises to Chuck? I love him! Yes, he's been a fool—I know that! But no matter what he's done, I know You can forgive him, so can I. He's my husband, and I know we can get through anything with You. You could stop this, turn him around to do the right thing!

What are You doing? What possible good can come of this? You can see what I cannot—what would You have me to do? Jesus, I can't stand this much pain much longer. It's like a broken leg of the heart. And Chuck never took over this business of his! What was the whole point of even

*starting it? I believed I was doing Your will! My cup is
totally empty, far from overflowing. Psalm 23 was written
by David about surrender, not circumstances. So, Lord, only
You can fill this cup I hold out to You. I'm a colossal mess,
but I can thank You, Lord, that I'm Your mess! I'm Your
child and totally dependent upon You. Please light my path
and fill this cup.*

Prayers as I drove were repetitious, as if the Lord couldn't hear me the first time. After a few hours, I realized I was the only one speaking. Pouring out can only last so long. Silence was a little relief. Prayer is two-way. I had asked the Lord a million questions and not bothered to listen for a single answer. I asked His forgiveness and vowed to listen.

The drive home, which was more than familiar, was to be unique. I saw the scenic western landscape as though for the first time. The wide-open desert panoramas were truly the much-needed big picture, a beautiful and a peaceful, unhurried reminder of God's glory, His presence. Soaking in striking visuals served to color the moment, allowed me to take deep healthy breaths, and open my heart to receive from the Creator of all I could see.

I nearly laughed as I suddenly remembered the frequency with which the Lord had to remind the Israelites of what He had done for them, freeing them from slavery. He might as well have said, "Annie, remember, I brought you out of Egypt." I thought about the greatest gift I had ever received for quite a while.

> *Jesus, I'm here only because of You and Your purposes
> for my life. You tell me I can be confident of this, that You
> began a good work in me and will carry it on to completion
> until the day of Christ Jesus. (Philippians 1:6)*

His words were perfect timing. I knew He was giving me perspective. Dad was raised to know the Lord for his first twenty-one years. I began thanking Jesus through my tears of deep gratitude for

God's Word embedded in my heart. I knew His Word was speaking to me.

> *Annie, your father also was included in Christ when he heard the message of truth, the gospel of his salvation. When he believed, he was marked in Christ with a seal, the promised Holy Spirit, a deposit guaranteeing his inheritance…neither death nor life, neither angels nor demons, neither the present nor the future, nor any powers, neither height nor depth, nor anything else in all creation, will be able to separate your father from the love of God that is in Christ Jesus our Lord.* (Ephesians 1:13–14, Romans 8:38–39)

The Lord reminded me of truths I could count on. He doesn't lie. I couldn't help smiling knowing He was speaking truth to me. And I was so grateful He put truth in my heart. It was right there when I needed it most. I thanked Him again for Andrea's influence in my life. I needed only to sit quietly in His company and listen.

> From my holy dwelling I am a father of the fatherless and a champion of widows. (Psalm 68:5, CSB)

Comfort flooded me as only He can do. I knew that Mom was really in good hands. His presence was so real I nearly looked to the passenger seat to see if He had buckled His seat belt.

> *Oh Jesus, thank You for Your faithful presence. Please know I love You, whether I feel You or not. Forgive my emotions that would consume me if it were not for You. I know that I cannot trust them. My cup was empty, not because my world is shaking but because I jetted into my own fearful little self. Not like I even thought about my knee-jerk natural reaction! The deeper into me, the darker it got. You didn't move, I did. Whatever lies ahead is in Your control, not mine or anyone else's. Lord, forgive my unholy lag. I know only*

You will help me be more fully in Your presence. My spirit must be smaller, Your Spirit must be bigger. Your spiritual truths move me to stand on the Rock—You. Thank You, merciful Jesus! Amen."

Chuck moved out while I was in Albuquerque and wanted a separation. Many reasons drove me to fight with every cell of my body to keep the marriage, but none greater than my belief that we were violating God's will: a sacred promise we made to live a Christ-centered marriage till death do us part. I could do nothing about the loss of my father or the stadium, but I could focus all my attention on a marriage quickly fading, on a man I loved. As driven as I was to hold the marriage, Chuck was equally resolved to abandon it. With each rejection, I would regroup, calling on God's strength, never wavering in my goal or trust that my Father in heaven was leading.

When he dodged my phone calls, I sent letters pleading for reconsideration and reconciliation. I would have done anything. And nearly did. Much of the time he was traveling in Europe on business, so I sent email letters. Love letters. Letters that counted one hundred ways in which I loved him. Letters that recounted the best times and the victories in the marriage. Letters that shared insights gained from books I was reading about codependency. Letters that confessed my contributing behaviors to a failing relationship, asking for forgiveness. Letters giving forgiveness for infidelity. Letters begging to meet in a counselor's office. Letters offering wonderful travel destinations to escape the ugly reality of where we were.

Most letters pointed to the Lord as our hope and surrendered our tangled mess to Him. Over a period of eighteen months of separation, I wrote hundreds of letters. I wrote a letter to the assigned judge four months before the pending divorce proceeding, to plead that he would require counseling and a period of reconciliation. I knew it was a political hot topic and hoped a compassionate judge could find a way.

Then in the courtroom on the day of the divorce, following three hours of deliberation to divide our earthly possessions, the judge asked me if I believed the marriage could not be reconciled. I cried out, "No, it *can* be reconciled! Pleeeeeeeease, make him go with me to a counselor!" My last pathetic effort to save our marriage failed.

Eighteen years dissolved when the judge said to my husband, "Your divorce request is granted." He got the divorce he wanted—in spite of my extended efforts, love, and his ignoring the will of God.

In retrospect, I thought my obsession to hold on to the marriage might have been a sickness, but I was told it was faithfulness. Faithfulness to promises made to Chuck and to God. I wasn't willing to break them or excuse them away, regardless of what Chuck did. The more obstacles I encountered, the harder I fought; the more counter resolve I met, the stronger mine grew. But then suddenly, the marriage was over. To hang on from that point forward would be sickness, not faithfulness. Turning that kind of love effort off like a water faucet wasn't going to happen overnight. I wanted to, but it just wouldn't turn off. The loss carried intense feelings that had to be understood and dealt with—grief.

There was no joy in divorce. I did not contribute to the divorce though I played a part in the failings of the marriage. This was totally different from the end of the marriage with Blake. Nothing inside me felt like anything apart from failure. The feelings of failure in marriage flooded everything else in my life. Nothing was right. My head said I must trust in God's purposes, for what I was living was not the end of the story. My heart ached so badly I could barely hear my head.

My head said I was a precious creation of the Lord God Almighty, with purpose and value. My heart saw ashes so deep I was too weak to even crawl out of them. The air was thick and weighty, pressing down. The pressure intensified. Ashes turned dense then to heavy water when thoughts of Dad poured in also. I looked up; I *was* the water spinning around and down the bathroom drain. I fought back, but I spun faster. I lost peripheral vision, out of control, spiraling. Pressed down beyond my strength to hold my head up. Powerless, I couldn't breathe. I dropped the ice cream cone into my lap that I had been frantically eating in my parked car—a pitiful effort to console myself. I screamed to God for air, but barely a whisper came out.

This was my second marriage down the drain, no irony in the metaphor I physically experienced as a panic attack. And how appropriate that it was raining while I sat sobbing in the car for hours. Light turned to dusk when I finally drove home.

Calling Andrea would have deteriorated rapidly to more crying and being unable to speak. So I wrote her a letter before dawn the next morning.

Dearest Andrea,

Yesterday, I lost Chuck for sure. Final and irreversible. My second failed marriage. I feel horrible shame in addition to all the loss. I will survive; the Lord promises to hold my hand, even when I let Him down. In my inmost being, I know He did not will this divorce, but He allowed it. I can't imagine why, but He knows.

I have a friend, so profound she lets me call her sister. She not only still loves me, but she has also loved me through the ugly of it all. And she accepts my love. Thank you, Andrea, for the rich love you give. So do my children. I have been especially difficult for Hanna in the past eighteen months—she has been the closest to the storm.

Tomorrow is the birthday of my first child, born without life in 1966. I only carried him seven months, but his loss was the first huge pain life dealt me—beyond my imagination. My parents lived in France, no relatives in town. I was young in a marriage that lacked the depth or intimacy to share so much emotional chaos…and so began an adult life that would be punctuated with similar themes of curve balls, left turns, and losses integrated with happiness, great joys, and blessings. Life in the adult lane.

My soul hungered for a spiritual life even then, for knowledge and wisdom to raise healthy children, and for love to be found in dear friendship that was lacking in family. The Father held me even before I knew Him. God was enough then and now. He has not abandoned me and still loves me. Being without Chuck is a place I never wanted to be, but already I can see I will not face the bitterness that followed divorce from Blake. All the letters I sent to Chuck begging him to come home were written from a place of love and forgiveness, a place with the Lord from which I can begin healing.

I have come to understand suffering far better than when he left, not a goal we ever set for ourselves. I understand my Lord and His ways better. And I know a lot more about myself. I have found a deeper love and acceptance from Jesus, friends, and children than I ever thought possible—quite a distance to come from when I saw myself as unlovable. So I *am* richly blessed. So much I wanted to tell you. I wish words were enough, but they're just a start. I thank God I will have eternity to share love and friendship with you—only then will we truly know how rich these relationships are.

The Lord has my back. He holds my hand. I thank Him that He used you mightily to hold my hand through such long, difficult months. And He goes before me. He will fight for me. Nothing is outside His reach to redeem. I only wish it didn't hurt this bad. Again, I can thank Him, just knowing that grieving is temporary. I haven't even begun to grieve the loss of Dad. But this season will not go on forever.

I love you, sister.
Annie

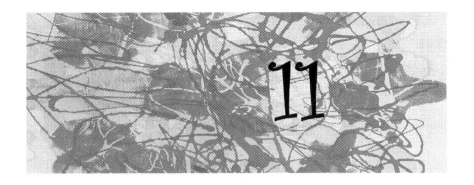

Holy Healing

The first little bits of early morning light were just starting to illuminate the world—famous, natural outdoor theater carved out in the middle of jutting rock. More than twelve thousand five hundred people crammed into Red Rocks Amphitheater just hours earlier for a popular rock music concert on a beautiful Colorado summer evening. Each seat enjoyed a spectacular wide and high view from the foothills overlooking the city of Denver. If the seats could speak, they would tell stories of performances for the past one hundred years, of every kind of artist from the Beatles to the Gaither gospel singers. But this one was different. Maybe they called this particular group Widespread Panic because of what their fans experienced when they discovered what they left behind: jackets, sweaters, sweatshirts, shoes, coolers, blankets, lots of blankets, cameras, binoculars, CD players, programs, and their clothes for crying out loud! Not to mention the voluminous food mess of nacho cheese, popcorn, peanut shells, soda and beer cups, hotdogs, pizza, in all manner of full, half-full, empty, upside-down, crushed, mixed, smeared, and some partially digested. Oh yum! Not one square inch was unadorned.

Most events left huge messes, but this blew past all prior experiences. This would have outdone even my brother's bedroom, which I recalled Mother's words describing as "Satan's finest work of art." Turning the lights on caused the skunks and raccoons to pause briefly from their glutinous gorging, but our presence didn't bother them a bit. There were more of them than us. I had only forty people, and the supervisor assigned for this project was a no-show. My best supervisor, Miguel, and a crew of forty were working a different job site, were scheduled to begin in two hours.

I was experiencing my own personal version of Widespread Panic. We had to have it all cleaned up and pretty in four hours—per contract agreement. The seating area was only part of the story. We also had huge parking lots, steps, walking paths, strewn with the same irrational quantity of trash. The word *litter* was woefully inadequate. Restrooms looked more like terrorists' training grounds. A stage, dressing rooms, staging areas, everyplace touched by attendees and performers made a statement that was the utter antithesis of order and cleanliness. My mother would not have remained vertical at the sight I was surveying. Someone would be performing CPR on her. Nor could she have adequately prepared me for something like this. However, this was not the time for reflection, blaming, or even the tiniest thought astray from "four hours to clean this eyesore and forty people to do it."

Not one person of the group of forty could speak English. My Spanish was limited to cleaning vernacular, counting, Mexican food, and large sweeping international body gestures. I considered letting the skunks and raccoons finish the job, but then that was just the food. We all spoke *very dirty* in unison. "Muy, muy sucio!" As I began directing initial efforts in different operations, I reminded myself that this business was as much ministry as business. These were faithful employees to show up at 5:00 a.m. and not run at the first sight of cleaning such a trash holocaust.

I thought about my costs to clean the site and knew I would lose money. We would not finish by nine o'clock—not even close. I joined in the effort, threading numerous large trash bags through my belt like the others. Choosing a grassy area next to the steps ascending the entire length of the seating area, I began to work my way from top to bottom. The object was to fill the bag quickly by hand, picking and stuffing as much trash as possible. Tie the bag, leave it, and fill the next. Others were assigned to collect the bags later. Our men followed with power blowers strapped on their back to remove the smallest of debris. Last, washers worked in the limited areas in which we were permitted to use water under conservation restrictions.

My work area was somewhat distanced from the groups systematically "picking" the seating area. I could see them. As cool as the early morning was, it took very little effort to work up a sweat, set a pace, and lose myself in personal thoughts. I was overwhelmed by failure, spiritually fatigued, and fixated in thinking, *What could I have done that I didn't do, and what did I do that I shouldn't have done?* The failed marriage outcome consumed everything else in my life. I felt like a homing pigeon with no place to land; flying was getting harder and harder. It was easy to see the parallel between the state of my life and the cleaning disaster I was facing that dawn.

Every step became a prayer as I fought to maintain outward emotional composure. Tears were poised to spring out like a break in a water main all the time, no matter where I was. Low-level nausea was ever present. Talking with God bubbled out as petitions for guidance, intervention, forgiveness, understanding, provisions, mercies, healing, wisdom, on and on. These were so numerous and scattered that I was certain even God would not be able to make sense of my prayers fraught with attention deficit disorder. Prayers were springing at Him like a popcorn machine at its most productive moment.

That's when I saw it—the money. Unlike many others, I never found money. Maybe the occasional penny or dime. But this was paper. Wow, a dollar! I had just reached the bottom of a serious pile of trash jammed up in a drainage runoff trough. The money was wet with beer. I had to pull away other paper stuck to it. *What on earth?* I couldn't move. I was holding a $100 bill! In one quick motion, I glanced over at the others to make sure no one was watching, slipped the money into the back pocket of my jeans, and bent over for the next piece of trash.

This is mine! Isn't it, Lord? Who would I turn it in to? Post a sign, "If you lost $100 last night, just call me to claim it"? Right! How long would $100 sit in a lost and found? No, it's mine! If it were not so, Lord, You would not have put it in my path. What a blessing! Wow! I turned thoughts to thanking God for such a neat thing.

> *Father, You have timed this so perfectly! But You knew that. It has been a long time since I have splurged and bought something unessential. Treat my kids to a dinner out! You are so good. All the time.*

These thoughts and prayers were clearly more fun than the ones I was having just a minute earlier—heavy grief thoughts that had taken up residence in my mind, nearly paralyzing me. There simply were no other thoughts despite my continual efforts to focus on other things. Amazing how a gift from God in our path could change things in an instant! I spent the money twenty-five different ways before I filled the next forty-four-gallon trash bag, which took all of three minutes. Then I began to wonder why I was so clandestine in not wanting others to know about my secret gift. *My* secret blessing!

Again, I asked the Lord if this were truly *my* blessing. My thoughts moved immediately to how much more I have than all forty of these workers. Collectively. I knew many of their personal stories. Working for me was a boon for them. The nature of the contract required they be paid above-average wages. I could only employ them when our event centers had an event—which was not every day all year long. Some weeks were very busy, some bone dry. Regular full-time dependable work was not feasible. Most of these people competed fiercely to be high on our call list when business needed them. Competing meant working harder than others—showing up no matter what, trying to understand my lousy Spanish. I started to think about them individually. And how they were deserving of more than I could give them.

Noel would strap a heavy blower on his back, walk down killer steep grassy embankments, and blow away debris that could not be cleaned any other way. Our contract did not even expect us to clean these areas. Noel would be classified as unskilled labor by Department of Labor statistics, but watching him lead a group of blowers in formation, systematically removing debris from seventy-six thousand seats of an NFL stadium, was observing an art form.

For years, Guadalupe and her husband cleaned nightly until after midnight in one of our dirtiest manufacturing facility contracts. The couple was among my longest-tenured employees, reliable and consistent. No one else could lead a group in arena restroom cleaning like Guadalupe and complete the quality job in record time. She worked on both sides of my business.

Gregorio was transportation for many others, never failing to fill his van and arriving on time. Many workers did not have transportation, or if they did, it was not reliable. Buses did not take people to amphitheaters on the outskirts of town by 5:00 a.m. Our cleaning locations and hours of operation were not "public transportation friendly." As a result, transportation was a major obstacle for even the best of workers.

Rogelio was a bottomless pit of energy; he was fast. I depended on him to set a pace for everyone else in sight of him. Beatriz had an attitude that was infectious with laughter, optimism, and encouragement for others. Juan needed very little guidance. Once a job was finished, he took initiative to begin another and take a few others with him. He was able to anticipate my next move. Ambrosio was the mechanical problem solver. There was nothing he couldn't fix in a jam, with duct tape and a rubber band. I depended on him as did his coworkers. They all were great workers. Many had received bonuses and recognition for their special efforts.

They lived on very little. I had driven any number of them home, following late-night stadium cleanups in very cold weather. Adequate coats, gloves, and hats were in short supply. I knew as many as eight men would sleep on the floor of one room, sending the better part of their paychecks to their families in Mexico. Others were trying to eke out a new life in a new country with daunting language barriers and an economy and culture that could be overwhelming. They had dreams of education for their children, a home someday to call their own, a bank account, and citizenship in America, a better life: the American dream.

But for now, a splurge to them meant to buy an air mattress to sleep on. It was not difficult to begin thanking the Lord for what I had—a home with nice furnishings, cupboards full of food, clothing, adequate coats, and boots. I had a bank account with some money in it, reliable transportation, and an education. A healthy body and healthy grown children, loving children. Goodness! I had my own business, great employees, great friends, an awesome church. Wow!

I wasn't too far down the list talking to Him when I heard Him say, "Pass the blessing."

"What? You mean the money?"

"Yes, the blessing in your back pocket."

"Oh, that blessing."

The remainder of the morning was overshadowed by a delightful mission. I looked at each employee a little differently.

"Lord, is it him? Is it her? How do I do this? What is the selection criteria?"

All employees started at the same time each morning, but they ended their shift at somewhat different times according to the last operation they were assigned. It would be first thing the next morning before I would have the opportunity to pass the blessing. We would clean up after Widespread Panic again; they would "perform" for the next two days.

By the time I wrapped things up at ten o'clock, I could have given the $100 to any one of forty people. What a beautiful job—collectively and individually! My feelings of gratitude and respect for them had never been stronger. And I was glad that Miguel would supervise the next day. I vowed never again to schedule the no-show lowlife supervisor who left me hanging that morning. Disparaging thoughts of him were quickly replaced with the reminder that I would not have found the $100 or enjoyed the morning in such an unplanned way had the shift gone as planned.

Getting to work before Miguel was tough to do. He had an annoying habit of arriving early, like thirty minutes early some days. My mother had told me since I was big enough to propel forward on my own little legs, I would be late for my own funeral. An early arrival for me was tantamount to learning Japanese. But I wanted to catch him before he got things started. Explaining my intentions to him, he fell right in step with me as we walked up the steep hill together in the dark from our parked cars at four forty. Briefly, I explained my incredible find the day before and plan to give it to someone that morning.

I needed Miguel's bilingual skills to interpret because I wanted to say things to the whole crew using language beyond my limited cleaning Spanish. More importantly, Miguel needed to understand why he would not be receiving the gift. His performance was a different matter—one that his frequent bonuses addressed and conveyed how much I valued him. This was meant for a different purpose. Though I had identified the person to receive it, I refrained from telling Miguel before telling the others.

Slowly, people began to arrive; Miguel signed them in and let them know I wanted to have a few words with them before we started. Some sat down and waited in the first few rows of the amphitheater; others stood by the rail and talked in small groups. As they gathered, I focused my attention on Leobardo, who was standing with Gregorio and Rogelio. What a quiet strength he had. I did not know how long ago this man had lost so much use of his right side, but it had been some time. Maybe a stroke, maybe an accident, a disease, I didn't know. His walk was slowed, his right leg an effort to pull along, his atrophied right arm and hand tucked in close to his body to be less obvious to others.

The smile he wore on his face was much easier to focus on. His smile said far more about him than his body that didn't work quite right. His general health was a challenge as well. There were a few days he would arrive in Gregorio's van scheduled to work but stay the day in the van, not well enough to work. He did not want to be counted as a "no-show," diminishing his chances for future work. On the days he worked, he was remarkable. He found ways to compensate for a diminished right side, ways that added up, making him a valued worker.

He insisted that Miguel assign him a blower job, which was one of the more physically demanding jobs. Once the larger pieces of trash were handpicked and bagged from the top portion of the seating area, five men would strap the gas-fueled blowers on their backs and begin working their way down from the top in a systematic routine, blowing the smaller pieces of waste. They would bunch together in tight formation, like jets in an air show, blowing the debris across five rows to another, whose job was to sweep up the collection, bag it, and remove it while the team walked back, blowing the next rows to the other side.

Leobardo had found a way to weave the hose of the blower around his withered right arm while supporting and directing it with precision from his left side. The gas blowers grew hot and heavy on the men's backs as the summer day heated up early. Leobardo worked twice as hard to keep up with the pace of the team. By the end of the operation, he looked as though someone had turned a hose on him. And he was grinning about it.

When the last of the employees had arrived, I called for their attention. I thanked them for such a great job the day before, described a few modifications in operations that Miguel and I had discussed that would help us to complete the momentous job more efficiently on the second day. Then I told them I wanted to relate something personal. I shared with them that I believed I lived a very blessed life. That God was good and I was blessed to know Him. Methodically, I listed some of the most obvious blessings that flooded my mind the day before: a business, great employees, my health, a home, wonderful children, a life full of God's purpose and meaning.

It was then I explained that early the previous day, while working in the grassy area near the south stairs, I was shocked to find money. I told them how much. Told them I knew the find was a gift from the Lord, a precious blessing. I led them with me as I shared my excitement over receiving this blessing—and on to the next realization that I was to pass the blessing, the money was not mine to keep. Every eye, every ear gave me riveted attention. I saw a desperate hope in each face. I knew $100 would be huge to any one of them. It took no Spanish translation to English to understand their faces.

I paused to consider the mistake I might be making—to delight one but disappoint thirty-nine other people. One man in the seating area called out that he had lost $100 yesterday and thanked me for finding it. Others laughed and immediately joined in, claiming it was theirs, many voices calling out they had lost money. We all laughed. But it wasn't really a light moment. This was nervous laughter. Anticipation was thick, and the dawn hung heavy as eyes darted through the bits of light to learn if this blessing were to be theirs. I had only moments to send up a frantic SOS prayer for rescue. My good intentions were tanking before I even got the intended recipient's name out of my mouth.

Stalling, it was the opportune time to thank many of them in the presence of their coworkers, for individual efforts they had made, meritorious of reward and attention. Most knew my gratefulness. Many had received previous recognition and bonuses. As I thanked them and shared with them how difficult it was to select just one to receive this blessing, I was having a dual conversation with the Lord.

Lord, what do You have in mind? I'm really on the hot seat here! I got into this and now wonder if I am not going to do more damage than good. Did You want to single one out and just pass it to them quietly, telling them to accept it confidentially? How long would that take before they all knew? Did I misunderstand? Was I not to pass this for Your honor and glory? Please, Father, I could use some help!

Funny time to think about an animated fish named Nemo, but words Dory said to Nemo in *Finding Nemo* came to mind when things got hairy on their underwater journey. I heard, "Just keep swimming, just keep swimming."

So I kept going, each face earnestly beckoning me to choose them. I told them there was one person who lodged in my mind. One who put forth such an exemplary strength of character. One who worked quietly for no special reward, just because he wanted to do the very best job he could. To do that, the cost for this person was greater than for the rest of us. And he did it every time he showed up.

Leobardo was standing against the rail only three steps away from me. He was perhaps the only one not looking expectantly at me; his gaze was fixed on the task at hand, the monstrous amount of trash we would remove that day. Startled, he turned toward me when I placed my hand on his shoulder.

As I said, "Leobardo, *we* want to pass this blessing to you." Thirty-nine people rose to their feet, clapping hard and with heart. They just kept clapping as Leobardo looked utterly stunned. He looked at me, then out at all his coworkers. He grew teary. Forty people had passed the blessing, not just me. Each one had wholeheartedly given their hope and blessing to him.

My prayer thoughts flooded.

> *Lord, You are amazing! Look what You have done with a beer-soaked $100 bill! Thank You, thank You, Father, that I got to be a part of this. You are awesome! How I love You! Please, let no one miss that You orchestrated this!*

I could not speak with authority to what the $100 did for Leobardo or for the other thirty-nine people who were present that special morning, but I can speak to what it did for me. It turned my mind from what I had lost, didn't have, and fears of what might be lost to a solid spotlight on what I did have. The $100 moved my focus from self to others. My pain was interrupted as I stood amazed, observing answered prayers of both days, blessing me with comfort in my mourning, bestowing a garment of praise instead of a spirit of despair (Isaiah 61:3). Healing was underway as the Lord was leading the way. Pulling out of the parking lot at nine fifteen that morning, I prayed praises.

O Lord, yes! Your ways are different for sure. Yes, I live a blessed life for sure. Your Word calls Your ways higher, better. They are not the same as ours. The same Book also tells me that I'll never understand them. Well, how could I? They are supernatural! Only You wrap blessings in garbage! But I can know Your character. I read about it, and I've most definitely experienced it today. You are faithful, wise, loving, powerful, forgiving, just, tender and kind, generous, giving. I could go on and on, which I did! You have asked me to trust You, meaning Your character. I don't have to understand Your ways to trust You. I do.

I know, as Your child, I am not spared pain. In fact, I understand I am to expect suffering in this world (John 16:33, CSB). The purposes of suffering are complicated and not fully explained, but You have told us enough for me to trust You for the unknown part of my pain. If it were not for You, Your steadfast love, I would have lost my mind. You sustain me, hold me, give me hope, and I know You will get me through this. You deliver on Your promises! It is in Your precious name, Jesus, I pray. Amen.

Dave was in terrible shape—suicidal. The leader of the divorce-recovery class at church asked if I would reach out to him. He was a businessman attending the class but not a believer. Dave's wife of thirty-five years walked out the day after his birthday. He lost a costly piece of business, worth millions of dollars, in the same time frame. The two were not connected in cause, but in terms of loss—they were, at least to Dave. He missed the money more than his wife and said so. His financial loss represented half his total worth. He was still wealthy, but devastated.

It wasn't as though I could relate to Dave. Goodness! I had hope. He did not. We were light-years apart in just about anything we valued. The leader thought because we were close in age and both owned businesses, I might be able to help. The Lord thought so too, but for different reasons. At the time, I thought our leader might as well have paired me with Warren Buffett on his worst day. I didn't know what kind of mindset Mr. Buffett had, but despite Dave's outwardly civil composure and obvious intelligence, he was a proud, cynical pessimist and a self-diagnosed narcissist.

Daily, I connected with him. Most days he didn't even get out of bed before 1:00 p.m. When he didn't answer his phone, I pounded on his door. We would walk around a small lake on adjacent property and talk. We'd talk at his kitchen table. I took him to see my pastor and they talked. My central talk theme was the hope I had that he didn't. His topics nearly always found their way to money. Why he would talk with me at all was definitely the God part.

After hearing the same repetitious complaints on one walk, I asked, "So, Dave, what would make you happy?"

"Winning the $72,000,000 lottery tomorrow."

I laughed, knowing him well enough to know even that sum would not make him happy beyond the moments of initial news. He did not understand that his emptiness could not be filled with money.

"You laugh, but have you ever bought a lottery ticket?"

I was surprised by the conversation directional change. "I don't see the relevance."

"Oh, Miss Holier-Than-Thou has never bought a ticket, but probably judges me that I do!"

"No, Dave. I'm certainly not your judge! My perspective is different. I see it as wasting hard-earned money. I would rather put money to something I think needs it, something worthwhile. I just learned this week, $30 will feed and house an orphan for a month in Africa. In my book, to be part of supporting a child is worthwhile.

Chances of you being struck by lightning are greater than your winning that lottery tomorrow."

"If there's a God like you say, He could let me win the lottery. First, I have to buy the ticket, and I plan to buy a bunch before tomorrow."

"If you're counting on God, you only need to buy one ticket." The second I said it, I regretted it.

"Ahaaah!" His retort was instantaneous. "So *you* buy a ticket if you have so much faith and then split your winnings with me because I thought of it!"

"Oh, Dave!" I laughed again. "The Lord knows money isn't what makes any of us happy. He's trying very hard to tell you that." The topic was a perfect segue to tell him the biblical teaching of Jesus. "No one can serve two masters. Either you will hate the one and love the other, or you will be devoted to the one and despise the other. You cannot serve both God and money (Matthew 6:24, CSB). God loves you and wants you to love Him back."

Dave couldn't wait for me to finish talking to say what he wanted. "I challenge you to buy just one lottery ticket!"

As I left the grocery store that evening about eight o'clock, while walking to my car, juggling a few plastic bags, purse, wallet, and a lottery ticket, I stopped dead in my tracks staring straight up at the dark sky.

> *O Lord, I just asked You to give me $72 million dollars, and*
> *I don't even have a plan for what to do with so much money.*

As reluctant as I was to accommodate Dave's challenge, I had just bought my first ticket, reasoning my act might somehow get me on the same page with him. Maybe he would actually listen.

Lord, I definitely got the cart before the horse. I have twenty-four hours to put a plan together. Please forgive me, I'll get back to You with something as soon as I can.

By noon the next day, I had little yellow post-it notes stuck all over my dash, visors, console, gear shift, and passenger seat of the car, resembling an explosion of 3M three-by-three notes. Visiting customer sites and delivering supplies took me all over the city. Multitasking wasn't an option, but a requirement. Each little note was another idea for spending $72 million. By the time I got home, little time remained before the drawing when a winner would be announced. I knew exactly what I had to do.

Information from each note was entered into an Excel spreadsheet. The math I set up allowed for the deduction of taxes and distribution of every remaining dollar. As I pushed against the deadline, excitement stirred. The money was going many different places, some I knew personally, but many I did not. The filtered thought was, *Will this cause the Lord to smile?* I set up accountability in the plan, a board of directors that would have to approve the distribution and administration of funds, even for the education of my grandchildren and greats to come. Part of the money would be designated for building efforts to grow the money, to perpetuate the funds for years to come. Some of the recipients who would need the oversight of a board were to be orphans in Uganda, Africa.

Satisfied, I pushed back from the keyboard and reflected on what had happened in the last twenty-four hours. For a one-dollar lottery ticket, I had set my personal gears in motion looking ahead, dreaming, planning, wanting to please my Lord. Exhausted in the best possible way, I went to bed not waiting for the televised announcement of a winner. Crystal clear in my mind was I won my personal lottery. This was a gift from the Lord, a redemptive gift, a healing gift I was all too pleased to receive. No doubt I slept with a smile.

"You got all that out of one lottery ticket?" Dave looked at me incredulously.

"Dave, I've been trying to tell you, life is so full when you have a relationship with your Creator. You are missing all this, but you don't have to."

"You live in a different world. I wouldn't know where to start," he mumbled.

I sensed a pensive mood. "Listening would be a great place to start. The Lord speaks to those who seek Him, who open their eyes and ears. Do you want to hear Him?"

"He's imaginary; money is real. Besides, narcissists don't change. I read the textbook."

"I didn't read that book. The one I read says I serve a God who can do anything. Would you be willing to come to church with me Sunday? You've already met Pastor Luke Pauley and liked him. What do you have to lose? You might hear God!"

We settled into one of the back rows. Dave sat slumped with arms folded across his chest, perfect body language to tell the world, "I really don't want to be here." But he was! I didn't drag him. He may not have wanted me to know, but his very presence was evidence of some kind of hope, seeking, questioning. The service might have been difficult for him, but he didn't speak. He watched other people, leafed through a hymnal from the back of the pew, and behaved as though he were not listening. I began praying for the dreadfully lost man on my left.

Pastor Luke was especially good. His messages were consistently good. If Dave got 10 percent out of the sermon, it would have been a success. Service nearly over, a member stepped up to the platform and announced the church was putting a team of volunteers together for a two-week mission trip to Hughes's Ugandan Ministries, serving orphans and widows of AIDS.

The short-term mission group would be building a home for Pat Hughes, among other things. Goodness! I even knew the woman when she was a member of our church. Ten years ago, she had followed her passion for orphans in Africa, moved there to begin a mission. The team would be leaving in four months. Anyone interested in going needed to speak with him.

I nearly jumped up on the pew to wave both arms! This was no coincidence, just three days after my personal lottery win. I abstained from such a display but knew this was a calling. Dave couldn't have known my insides were dancing, but what was going on inside him was evident. His eyes were big as saucers. The same dots I was connecting were speaking to him. He realized something very special was happening. A message just for him from God! Dave smiled at me.

I whispered to him, "God is not a figment of our imagination. He's real, He's here, He speaks, and He is love. I think you heard Him."

Whatever may have happened for a despairing man that Sunday morning evidently stayed in the church as far as I knew. The Bible speaks of those who meet Jesus and still choose to go their own way. In fact, He speaks of the extreme difficulty of the rich to choose Him as a priority over their wealth. Dave chose money. He broke my heart; I can't imagine what his choice did to the heart of our Lord! Somehow, Dave worked himself to a slightly less-desperate place. I chose Africa—to follow the Lord to higher ground. The time with Dave closed with a prayer as I left for Uganda.

> *Lord, thank You for Your ways. I love You so much. I would never have seen my healing in helping a person like Dave! But You did! I've done what I can. He is really Your project, and You have moved me on in amazing ways. I pray You will bless Dave and turn his heart toward You. He's so lost! Please, have mercy on Dave. Thank You for holding my hand and drawing me close. In Jesus's precious name, amen.*

Right but Not Righteous

Grieving, healing, and forgiving all go together. I didn't find shortcuts, but I would find ways to draw the processes out. Nothing about them was linear; however, both blessings, mistakes, and learning lay ahead much like an unmapped field, laden with beautiful wildflowers and land mines.

Friends recommended books to read, so many that I began a list, reading them in the order in which they were recommended. With the attention span of a gnat at the beginning, it took a while reading five books at a time. I learned I was no different from others, untrained in how to grieve, and frightfully vulnerable. When I could keep my eyes on Jesus, then He had much to feed me, ministering in countless ways.

Reading His Word every morning, journaling, faith-based music, sweet comforting cards and words of family and friends, devotionals, books, God winks, visual scenes of His glory, birdsongs, doggie cuddles, endless means. He was unlimited in the ways He made His presence known and delivered His promised comforting love.

"I would like for you to lead a home study of Rick Warren's book, *The Purpose Driven Life*. We will be doing this churchwide in the members' homes," a wise and compassionate friend asked me one day not too far into my grieving process.

"You're kidding me, right? I'm a mess! Your timing couldn't be worse. You expect me to behave like a leader of wiser people than me?"

"This study was made for you right now! Jump in and thank me later. Here's the book." She handed me a book—both title and author were new to me. "The people coming to your house will have their own book." A couple of years earlier, she had roped me into volunteer leadership in addiction recovery, which was yielding great results. I wasn't an eager responder then either, but knew the wisdom of not denying this woman's invitations.

The ten-week study was powerful, grounding all of us in fully knowing we were intentionally made and set in motion with purposeful life on this good earth. My sweet friend knew I would never request this kind of help, but badly needed. Teaching embeds a truth even more deeply than hearing. Perfect timing. But of all means the Lord used to heal me, none was greater than His Word. In addition to daily manna of the Word, He provided a Word study to dig out nuggets to protect mind and heart. Yes, He did all of that.

The herculean effort to draw Chuck back home during the separation was made more in love than in fear. Forgiving Chuck happened each time I asked him to come home. In God's hands, my efforts were not in vain (1 Corinthians 15:58, CSB). Forgiving myself, finding patience, healing, and waiting were the biggest challenges in my grieving process.

I would also love to claim that once learned, always learned. His loving patience *for* me produced patience *in* me, the kind Jesus has. What's not to want about that? Patience was essential in healing, grieving, and forgiving. I had to say yes to the Lord in ways I had not said before.

Grieving and healing were times in which I was shaped like no other. When completed, my feet were on higher ground than when grief began. How could I possibly refrain from praising Him for everything?

When I thought grieving was all done, it wasn't. When I thought it wasn't, it was. Doesn't make sense, I know. There came a time when my grieving turned to self-pity, which added a truckload of unnecessary pain. Unforgiveness, blame, pride, and self-pity went hand in hand to stall closure. The enemy told me these things were just all part of grieving. The Lord said not so. He calls these things sin. He tells us there is a time for grieving, but there is never a time for sin. I could be either a victim or a victor. The enemy won a victory whenever I was bigger than the Lord. Time and again, I would have to dig out of one of the enemy's grieving rabbit holes. Overwhelmed, I'd cry for help, and the Lord faithfully pulled me out. Repetition nearly wore me out.

> *Lord, I'm reminded of the word* tenacious *when I consider endurance or perseverance. The really strong stuff You value in our character that is needed to finish the race. Stuff that stands up no matter what the enemy throws at me. Stuff that defies what the culture might define as enough. Your Word tells me this is a race You've marked out for me. Mine is unique. I get that. The stuff needed to run my race will be different from races of others as well. I understand I'm lacking all the stuff needed, but You have deposited Your spirit within me to run. You are enough.*
>
> *Tenaciousness is never giving up. When I wanted to throw up my hands, everything grew dark as sorrow swept over me once again. A broken world was more visible to me than You were. But tenacious is like a puppy on a rag. The pup loses baby teeth in the process of hanging on, maturing in the process. He doesn't question—he gives the effort his all, just focused on hanging on. That stuff is the needed character for the race You have set out for me.*
>
> *You are tenacious! You never give up on me. You will never leave me nor forsake me. You never take Your eyes off me. Nothing can separate me from Your love. Thank You, Father, for who You are. Your tenacious faithfulness is*

unending, eternal. What You have done for me on the cross is beyond my comprehension. Nothing can derail You from accomplishing what You set out to do. My part? Just hanging on isn't enough. I'm not a puppy—I'm a child of the King. I will pick up my cross and follow You.

I do not want those who may be a part of my sorrow to miss the grace You pour out in my behalf. I pray that nothing I do, say, or how I respond is in vain. I pray they see You. In the power of Your name, I pray for Your strength. Amen.

The Lord provided the "strength that endures the unendurable and spills over into joy, thanking the Father who makes us strong enough to take part in everything bright and beautiful that He has for us" (Colossians 1:11–12, MSG).

"We're coming to visit you, cuz, in just a few weeks. Been wanting to do this a long time, but finally, we're gonna make it happen!" Eric caught me totally by surprise and sent me into wonderful anticipation.

"You know you will be in grave danger of being kidnapped! No amount of time will be enough. I'll just have to keep you." This was a man I dearly loved, far more like a brother I always wanted than a cousin. He and his wife were making a trip to see me in Denver, coming all the way from western Montana. Travel was infrequent for them, a major treat. I packed as much into the visit as I could.

At the age of nineteen, Eric had come to live with our family during my last year of high school. Fresh from small-town Montana, he had no clue what life outside his hometown might look like, except for summers spent on Grandpa's ranch in central Montana. Eric needed a fresh start following a medical obstacle that totally changed his planned direction. Mom's Montana roots and offer to help provided the opportunity he needed.

As teens, we shared the shock of life in a progressive state like

New York, even in an upstate city. The drinking age was eighteen, kids partied hard, everything seemed competitive, so fast, and Eric hadn't even signed up for the race. Nor had I. Dad was transferred from Cincinnati, Ohio, to Utica, New York, at the start of my senior year of high school. I left skid marks all the way in the move. As different as Eric and I were, we shared plenty.

Toward the end of their meaningful Denver visit, I believed attending a softball game of my grandson would be a family highlight. We'd see all three grandchildren one more time, Peter and his wife, and maybe Hanna would be able to make it. Well, it might have been great had Blake not been there. In a flash, the whole event was ruined. Why did I not know he was coming? Good grief! Eric was even thrilled to see Blake.

Forgetting Blake's offenses wasn't going to happen in this lifetime, though I no longer dwelled on them and the oldest of them certainly faded. I had forgiven him. The offenses since the divorce that most affected the kids were the hardest to forgive. Push/pull, choose, choose! The theme played out in endless scenarios. How contemptuously he treated Hanna at the same time favoring Peter, even as adults. Reports plunged me into painful cartwheels of the heart—heartwheels.

However, I was soon to learn the difference between forgiving and forgetting. How many years had it been? Thousands of offenses. Yet decades after the marriage ended, the anger and rage welled up in me while seated in the steel bleachers, as though all Blake's offenses happened just yesterday. I looked out over my grandchildren's green baseball playing field and watched the peaceful green grass release any peace the loveliness might have held.

Oh no, Lord! He is not off the hook! No way! He doesn't get a free pass just because time passes! In many ways, he's worse, not better, even though the kids are grown. No, not for all that he has done.

The aha moment of brutal honesty was a very long time coming. If denial had a color, I would have been sitting in a pool of ugly rusty brown as every pore of my body released all I had stored. Listening to Blake prattle on and on, with Eric as his captive audience, ratcheted my anger up even higher, first directed toward my son for telling his dad that Eric and Sandy would be at the game. Peter didn't even ask me if I wanted to share the family time. Didn't he care if it ruined the precious time with grandchildren and now the little remaining time with Eric? Didn't he realize how much each encounter with his family meant to me? Had Peter grown so dreadfully insensitive to the effects of his dad on me?

My reflections and anger turned to Jesus.

> *Oh Lord, am I supposed to pretend this man is someone he is not, to be his friend, because it would be convenient for everyone else? No! I'm done with pretending. Sharing all Christmases, Thanksgivings, and family birthdays. This man is not my friend; if he's not my enemy, who on earth could be worse?*
>
> *I drove Eric and Sandy thirty heavy-traffic miles to Peter's side of town to visit with my son, his wife, and my grandchildren at their ball game. Not to visit with Blake. And now Blake is hogging, dominating, stealing every dwindling minute of the ball game. Why did I come at all? What a waste! O Lord, this just isn't right!*

Blake's infinite capacity for boasting of himself resounded in my ears. Listening to rap music at an intersection loud enough to cause hearing loss had greater appeal. But what bothered me the most, in the red-hot moment, was that Eric had moved two rows down the bleachers and was engaged in the listening end of Blake's monologue—evidencing enjoyment!

Lord! Doesn't Eric know what a Jekyll and Hyde Blake is? Doesn't he know what the mean-spirited ex-husband has done to me? That person Eric's talking to is the very person who turned my life upside down, still does. Lord, how can this man continue to receive any respect from people I know and love? It's not right, Lord!

Of course, Eric knew. But he didn't understand. Eric had not seen Blake since the day we were married. He had no clue who the man really was. Oh my, what was the liar saying to Eric? I found Blake's spirit of licentiousness disgusting. He called it humor. He labeled wholesome as puritanical. His way of thinking was the real world; God was not needed. My world was sheltered, uninformed, outdated, and naïve. The self-appointed authority endeavored to teach his children to think the same. And anyone else who would listen to him. The past was a taboo topic for my kids, so his effect could not be overlooked. I had serious doubts they would ever know the truth, their thinking having been reprogrammed.

He still wore a white hat. I wore the black hat if I opened my mouth. Was it any wonder that after all this time, I still wretched at his moves?

No, Lord, he is not off the hook. Yes, he is accountable. To me! To You! He may be an atheist, but he will one day stand before You. The fool has tried continually to ruin my life, caused a lifetime of damage to his kids—doesn't anyone care? If they loved me, they would understand and care, or at least try!

I had been angry before in my life, but never with the intensity I felt staring out over the ball field. The more I thought about the cumulative injustices, the greater my emotional pitch spiked. Talking to the Lord escalated my rage. It was difficult to sit still—sunglasses at least hid part of my face.

Even today, the man is an alcoholic, he doesn't know truth from a lie, and he's a master manipulator. Why am I so alone in understanding what is sooo wrong? It's complicated and lengthy, but the story definitely has a right and wrong, a good guy and a bad guy, right, Lord? You know the whole thing, every sordid detail. Will there ever be an end to the pain of it all?

The thoughts I couldn't suppress caused a wellspring of fat, hot tears I struggled mightily to keep from rolling down my cheeks. *Friends don't want to hear the latest offense in the never-ending no-divorce epic saga anymore.* Eventually, I let them off the hook, told them there was nothing new; it was all in the past and forgiven. *Well,…it isn't as if I haven't forgiven him. Don't thousands of times, every way I know how, count for something?*

Thankfully, I kept my mouth shut as I stared ahead. The look on my face must have betrayed *some* of the ugly bile barely beneath the surface. *Good that no one is looking at me,* I thought. *Blake is the focal point. Christians are supposed to be forgiving, especially decades after the offenses.* I was practiced at intellectually attacking the problem of forgiving; I had forgiven him so many times. I just desperately wanted him to quit giving me new occasion to forgive him. Like right now.

My pastor's recent sermon on the topic of murder mingled with my exploding out-of-control thoughts. *Wow, that message was not coincidental.* I recalled how he spoke from Jesus's teaching on murder: You've heard it said to the people long ago, "Don't murder, and anyone who murders will be judged. But I tell you that anyone who is angry with his brother or sister will be judged. Again, anyone who insults his brother or sister will answer to the court. Whoever says, 'You fool!' will be in danger of the fire of hell" (Matthew 5:21–22).

The pastor taught about the path of anger as it rises up unimpeded—it is the perilous path to murder. Yes, exactly the rage I felt—the top of the ratcheting, escalating, deadly sequence of emotions I could barely contain looking out over the grass that was no longer a beautiful green. It was stinkin' red! Even the children weren't really visible. If I could have sent Bruce Willis to blow him up, I would have.

Sitting on a metal riser with unprecedented rising anger, crushing loneliness, and a growing sense of annihilating defeat, the thought rolled into my head like a bowling ball about to strike the tenpins.

> *This is so wrong, Lord! I am soooo wrong!* I'm *the problem.*
> *I have never forgiven Blake. And I judge him every time I*
> *think of him.*

The color of the baseball field screamed I hadn't forgiven. The spirit stirring inside me said I definitely had not. I had called him every nasty name in the book, judged him, and murdered him. In the moment, I *knew* in both heart and mind I had not been honest with myself or anyone else for decades. The good, bad, and ugly truth of unforgiveness had just moved to the brain's cerebrum, front and center—an aha moment of utter honesty, suppressed truth for many, many years.

"What's in the well comes up in the bucket" is biblically expressed as "Guard your heart, for everything you do flows from it" (Proverbs 4:23). My bucket of bitterness included serious unforgiveness that would rise in the form of judgment, anger, blame, even hate, now rage. As long-suppressed emotion rose up like biting bile while I looked out over the children's ball field, I knew all I had denied was as lethal as a heart attack if I tried to stuff the acidic volume back inside.

The Lord knew the truth and let me know. I had tried as hard as I could to forgive, but on my own steam, efforts only amounted to a lot of dirty huffing and puffing. Over and over, I repeated the epic truth confession that was covering my raging emotions like slurry on a forest fire. No more self-deceit. Then I heard His Voice speak from His Word.

"Annie, your struggle is not against flesh and blood, but against the rulers, against the authorities, against the powers of this dark world and against the spiritual forces of evil in the heavenly realms (Ephesians 6:12). I have already won the victory. Greater is He that is in you than he that is in the world (1 John 4:4). If I am for you, who can be against you? (Romans 8:31). Forgive this man and I will forgive you" (Matthew 6:14).

Words I knew well, but in the moment, I was seeing for the first time with my heart's eyes (Ephesians 1:18, paraphrased). They were personal, not just theological teaching. The Lord spoke to *me*, and I heard Him in my heart, mind, and soul. He turned me around.

All sin is against You, O Father! I have sinned against You and You alone (Psalm 51:4, paraphrased). *I have carried this rotting unforgiveness for years. Not just the damage done to me, but damage to others. How can I ask Your forgiveness for this? Your Word says I must not even ask until I have forgiven Blake.*

How could I harbor this so long, even forgive Chuck but not Blake? I've told myself so many lies, suppressed so many truths of Yours, denied or justified my own feelings. I have lived in such a selfish place, removed from the holy reality of it all—I've hopelessly lost my way in something so dear to You. The crucifixion of Your only Son was all about forgiveness. What have I done?

I've tried to hold him accountable to me! And others like Peter. Like I'm a kind of god! Goodness, I've judged, convicted, and sentenced! Only You can do that, and my guilt is what's bright red before me. I don't resemble You in any way. No, I look like the world around me that You are trying to save.

How I need You! Please, O Father, come and get me as You have so many times before. I feel so terribly unworthy, awful, alone. I have worked against You, not for You.

Never let me forget my own sin and Your forgiveness given in the darkest of all hours—the cross. You paid for all of mine, who am I to hold someone else accountable to me?

Teach me to forgive this man once and for all. To hate evil but not the person engaged in sin. He is Yours, just like I am. Precious. You love him every bit as much as You love me. I want to forgive him in Your love. In Your strength, not mine. For the sake of Christ. For the sake of my children. For the sake of Blake.

I thank You that You are a long-suffering God. I know that You have suffered far more than any of us can ever imagine because You don't want any of us to perish. I know You have Blake in mind as You say "whosoever." And me. And all mankind—no exceptions. Oh Jesus, yes, I forgive Blake. I do. I want to love him as You do.

Please, Lord, please forgive me. Amen.

Tears of relief fell, adrenaline subsided, composure began to return, and the grass turned green once again as the spirit of the Lord had grown bigger than my own. I knew I was in a momentous holy moment, a redemption never to be forgotten.

A little time later, I scooted down a couple of levels of seats to join the rest of the family.

The day oozed important insight for weeks. I could see that unforgiveness would sit indefinitely with no shelf life. It didn't evaporate with time or drown with alcohol. Just because we have bigger problems, it doesn't go away. It doesn't seep out of a Christian just because we love God, do good, or go to church. In fact, it fermented and rotted in its container, then would rot the container if left indefinitely.

Once I forgave Blake, I realized I had spent years blind to anything good about him. The remarkable qualities I once admired were still there, and the more mature man merited genuine recognition for professional and volunteer work he did in the community and even beyond. His heart for the less fortunate was evident. I also began to speculate about his devout Christian mother as she grew so ill with tuberculosis. With an unstable, alcoholic husband who was in and out of her life, surely she knew her children would be orphaned if she didn't survive. I knew if I were in her position, nothing would be more important to me than to make certain my children knew who Jesus was. Nothing! I would not rest until they understood and believed He was who He said He was.

Suddenly, I saw Blake as a lost lamb, very misguided, but nevertheless, one of His. How easy it would be for him to lose his way in the orphanage years. Memories of the abuse that he told me about still haunted me. Much damage he sustained explained, in part, the abuse I received in marriage.

Since then, he worked relentlessly trying to control everything around him, to make himself the man he wanted to be and anesthetize the pain he denied. Not so very different from so many others. But Blake had deep scars and secrets he had become practiced at covering. His "coping" skills were self-destructive and damaging to others. Still, he loved his children perhaps more than his own life. They had to see him the way he needed them to see him, as an overcomer, certainly not as a lost lamb.

I shuddered, with unexpected compassion, as I realized how much I could relate with his coping means that created a destructive Jekyll and Hyde. How dare I judge him. The only difference between us that really mattered was Jesus.

Soon after the children's ball game, a new and different thing happened in church during the Sunday morning service. Brian, our worship pastor, asked that we take out the blank piece of paper in our bulletins that Sunday and a pencil from the pew ahead. He asked the Lord to prepare our hearts for prayer. For five minutes of silence, we were to write a prayer of whatever the Lord stirred in our hearts.

Oh Lord, You alone are holy, worthy of our praise! You are faithful when I am not. You stir the spirit of my soul. Change my heart where I have allowed it to grow angry or bitter. Wash and purge any thoughts I harbor against others. Forgive me and give me Your grace, strength, and opportunity to forgive those who have sinned against me. Keep my heart in Your hands. Let me never be bitter. It's about You! Not me. Teach me to respond to You—not the world or the conflict that fills the days.

Thank You, Lord, for the pruning You have done, are doing today, and will do tomorrow. I commit my soul, my heart, my strength to Your purpose. Mold me, Father, keep my eyes on You; they are prone to stray.

Take these emotions that would steamroller me and turn them to intensity for You. I pray Your grace to love others as they are, flawed as I am. Let me serve them with Your spirit bigger than mine. Let me die for You each day, hour, and minute to be more like You.

Give me the passion You would grant for Your ministries and missions, Lord. I pray I don't get out in front of You as I'm inclined to do. Take my gifts and help me to use them wisely. You alone have loved me completely, filling me with love for others.

I want to obey You with all that I am. I want to live for You—to make You pleased, give You joy. I love You, Lord Jesus, and pray all things in Your name.

Amen.

What a joy and honor I found worshipping with others who love the Lord! To know my brothers and sisters were also broken and healing, not so different from me, just unique in their own journey. To know my life was on the same path as theirs, the Lord weaving our lives together and that we would spend eternity together. Experiencing joy and fulfillment many times along the way, sometimes together, but to know this isn't heaven, just a taste.

As I drove home, I pondered my guilty part in trying to make this place like heaven. I knew I couldn't be perfect or fix others, and I did not want to die trying. So thoughts turned to why I do find myself doing these things. *The finest I can do is submit to the Lord. He's my changer. Oh my, this will be especially difficult for me.*

My humanism, my way, apart from the Lord is a daily battle. Left to my own tendencies, I want to hold others accountable for the way they treat me, what they say, do, or don't do. Especially that part of the Word about treating others the way we want to be treated. My expectations get in the way, even more with brothers and sisters who are supposed to be like-minded.

> *Oh Lord Jesus, I need help here. Consciously or unconsciously, I think others should treat me the way I treat them or the way that You tell all of us to treat one another. I'm hurt when they don't. Depending on what it is, I can be incredibly hurt. Your crucial command just all goes south when I give the Golden Rule a tiny twist, expecting like treatment in return from others when I have loved them.*
>
> *When the unexpected happens in return, well, depending on how I respond, that's where You become a Light or everything goes dark. With my tiny human nature twist, the dark path carries judgment, self-service, maybe self-pity, anger, bitterness, and unforgiveness. The help I need is to put into practice what I know. This may be easy for others, but oh so hard for me. Then there's talking the problem over with others. Is that gossip or seeking wise counsel? Oh, I knew the answer to that before I even asked.*

"His spirit cannot be bigger than mine when I'm so focused on how wounded I am and how I need to fix a mess," I confessed my tendencies and offenses to Andrea not long after the historic Forgiving Blake Day.

"That's all the enemy's tar paper. You're missing the heart of God's second most important command." Andrea offered her wisdom despite being quite sick. "Love others exactly how He loves you, give it your all. That would be *all* others God brings to you. None of your own expectations, no judging, no justifying, no exceptions—just loving them as they are, no matter how they treat you.

"He placed difficult people in your life with purpose." Andrea spoke truth from her own experiences. Her life had been riddled with plenty of trying examples. Now, she was coping with her second diagnosis of breast cancer. "No doubt I'm a difficult person in someone else's life," she added as we both laughed. I couldn't imagine that she could possibly be a difficult person in anyone's life.

"The Lord shares His business with us—to forgive and love and get on with life. The Lord takes care of the judgment and justice part. Forgiveness may or may not change others, but it *will* change us. It changed me. Think of it like a dance

> Forgive them *when* they sin and He will forgive
> me. (Matthew 6:14, paraphrased)
> *How* I am to forgive? From my heart. (Matthew 18:35, paraphrased)
> If I don't forgive? My Father will not forgive
> *my* sins. (Matthew 6:15, paraphrased)

"Just hold on to knowing the strength and love to forgive, the desire, the genuineness, can *only* come from our Lord."

My Forgiving Blake Day was all I needed to testify to the truth my precious friend spoke. The joy in healing was unparalleled. "He [Christ] himself bore our sins in his body on the cross, so that we might die to sins and live for righteousness; by his wounds you have been healed. For you were like sheep going astray, but now you have returned to the Shepherd and Overseer of your souls" (1 Peter 2:24–25).

Never Too Late

I called my aging mother in Albuquerque to tell her I had booked her airline reservation to Denver. Explaining she needed to record the flight information, she set the phone down to find paper and pen to write. When she returned to the phone, I tried to continue. It quickly became apparent that she needed her hearing aids, as she was having difficulty hearing despite my repetition, careful articulation, and escalating volume.

"Put the phone down, Mom, and please take the time to find your hearing aids," I suggested. "I can wait."

After a lengthy silence, she once more came back to the phone. When I tried to resume, I was interrupted once again.

"Now, what have you done with my pen?" she asked.

"Mother, I'm in Denver and you're in Albuquerque," I responded.

"Well, there's no one else in this room," she said.

Trips to Albuquerque were happening more frequently—nearly every other weekend, I made the nine-hundred-mile round-trip drive. In many ways, Mother had already lost grasp of the fact that I was not local. She was trying to recover from a recent devastating break of the closest relationship of her ninety years, apart from my dad—my sister, Diana.

The falling out of such a strong, long-standing mother-daughter bond was an unprecedented trauma she was ill-equipped to handle. Over the years, Mom and Dad made no pretenses about which of their children they favored. Diana had long enjoyed the unchallenged favor of both. In my parents' senior years, the favoritism grew heavily shaded with dependency. In a single day, an atrocious quarrel resulted in broken trust. The relationship was severed. Mom's life jolted on a magnitude scale of a 7.2 earthquake.

She lived alone in a retirement facility enduring "alone" in ways she had never known. Dad had been gone three years. Macular degeneration had taken most of her eyesight, and her loss of hearing exceeded hearing aid technology by at least 50 percent. Her already heavy drinking increased significantly. One night, she fell in the dark trying to reach the bathroom. Bleeding stomach ulcers and long-term alcohol abuse literally pinned her to the floor for ten painful hours until she was discovered by concerned neighbors the next day.

Mom had outlived most of their many friends. Those remaining locally were infrequent visitors. The new relationships she had established in the retirement home comprised her day-to-day life. They shared meals together and lived in a close-knit community. Over a period of two years, three women were found in the morning, dead in their beds for no apparent reason. Residents were never to learn the rest of the story—they were left to speculate. The widely held conclusion was they had stockpiled medications, which if taken in large dosages, proved lethal. Daily my mother quietly contemplated a feasible path of departure from a life she no longer valued. I was unaware.

On a weekend trip to see her, I arrived Saturday in time to run some errands and do a little shopping with her. The shared time seemed to be a needed break even more than usual. We talked about her childhood in Montana, the stark contrast of today's lifestyle with simple pioneer like life on a homestead ranch. She told stories of her parents, husband, and some of her old friends. My visits with her were meaningful and clearly a highlight in her routines. Her grasp of my arm was stronger this time, and she remained closer.

She struggled on many levels that were evident, but expressing emotions was not something she knew how to do. In fact, I only saw my mother cry twice in my life. Once in my teen years and the second time would come later that evening. Even when her husband died three years earlier, she remained stoic in her resolve to hold tight her emotions.

Happy hour began daily at four o'clock in her apartment, preempting the decades-old tradition of five o'clock. I drank Diet Coke while Mom drank Jack Daniels on the rocks. Cheese and crackers accompanied the historic ritual. Watching was hard. Snacks were not enough food to offset the effects of liquor consumed on a 115-pound ninety-year-old frail frame. When we left for the dining room at six o'clock to join others, her speech was showing the effects of six ounces of alcohol, and her walker served multiple purposes.

Dinner and social time over, we returned to the apartment where drinking and talking continued. When her speech became difficult to understand, I suggested we call it a day. As we got ready for bed, she emerged from her bathroom still talking, wanting me to understand something important to her. I moved in very close and asked her to speak slowly. Shortly, I learned of the three friends who had recently died in their beds and her perspective on why. Her voice began to break as she reported they had done what Socrates did to take his own life, and she wanted to do the same.

Hearing aids on the counter in the bathroom meant this was mostly a one-way conversation. I wrapped my arms around her as she folded into my support and sobbed. Holding my broken mother while standing in the hallway for considerable time, I didn't move but eventually interrupted the silence. My mouth was an inch from her ear.

"Mom, I love you," I cried also. "More than you know." We stood silently for a while longer.

"You need sleep right now most of all, and then in the morning, we will resume this conversation. After breakfast, we are going to church. Right here in your apartment." Pointing to the little bistro table she had sitting in front of a sliding glass door, visible from where we stood, I asked, "Are you willing to come with me to church?"

She nodded in agreement and tried to collect herself. For the first time in my life, I tucked my mother in bed and kissed her good night. There would be many more to come, but the first rattled me down to my cell level.

Mom slept well. I did not, but the night was far from a waste. I prayed between naps until seven o'clock when I heard her up. She made no mention of the night before, nor did I. We met her circle of friends as usual for their continental breakfast routine. Mom talked and laughed as though nothing out of the ordinary had occurred nine hours earlier. Returning to her place, the day might have gone like any other Sunday for a woman who had lived a life with God in distant shadows, but this Sunday was not to be a day like any other.

"Shall we?" I gestured as we entered her apartment toward the little bistro table where I had placed my Bible before going to bed.

"Oh yes, I remember," she acknowledged then shifted her gaze downward.

Somewhat surprised at her recall, but mostly by her willingness to follow through, I guided her directly to the table situated in the morning sun. Seated, I placed one hand on the Bible and offered the other to Mom, inviting her to join me in prayer.

"I promise I won't sing," I said, impulsive words breaking the awkwardness, inspired words that joined us in laughter to begin our unorthodox church time.

What followed can only be described as the most precious time God gifted me to spend with my mother. I never opened the Bible, but my hand never left its cover. The holy book remained in the center on the small round tabletop, the unspoken reflection of the very presence of God, the heart of our discussion, the supreme authority in all scripture I quoted.

"I don't have a sermon to preach, nor am I a Bible scholar. But I can speak with confidence about what I know better than any other person—who the Lord is in my life and what He has done."

I spoke of my faith story with Him. How it began in 1976 in Albuquerque, at a time when I had come to the end of myself and every self-help or new age straw I had grabbed. How I was completely overwhelmed by circumstances at a crisis level, losing ground, and frightened.

"I remembered crying out to God that I needed help as I went to sleep one night. He sent a little boy to my door shortly after, with an invitation to church. I won't go into all the details of that, Mom, but in retrospect, there is no way I would have walked through the doors of that church had it not been for the little neighborhood boy. Ten Sundays later culminated with God's saving grace on Easter morning. Mom, I encountered Jesus, not just God the Father, God the Creator, but Jesus the Savior and Lord of my life.

"He poured out incredible blessings immediately following my decision to follow Jesus. He grew a career for me, born out of nothing and escalated beyond anything logical. His grace carried me over and over throughout turbulent years of foolish choices I made as a Christian and especially granting the strength to overcome alcohol addiction in a totally unconventional way—dependent upon *only* Him every step of the way."

I told her my belief that He wanted for my life to show others that *anything* is possible with Him. Just Him, He is enough. He protected my children in a dirty divorce that was unending. I spoke of God's character throughout, His underlying motive of love in everything He does, whether it's justice or mercy. How He changes us, teaches us, and gives us joy we can experience no other way. I explained He wanted her to know Him also.

"I want what you have," she interrupted me to say.

"The Lord heard you, Mom!" I spoke words packed in utter joy. "It's as simple as believing Jesus is who He says He is. Who is Jesus, Mom?"

"He's God's son."

"Yes, He is. You are absolutely right." I squeezed her hand.

"God the Father sent His Son Jesus to redeem our broken lives because He loves us. To save us from an eternity separated from Him."

"You mean hell?" she asked.

"Yes, the Word spells it out pretty clearly." We both glanced at the Bible under my other hand.

"We're all broken, Mom, because of sin. We're born with a sin nature. You didn't have to teach me how to lie." The example was a slam dunk and drew her smile.

"God wants us to love Him back, to know Him personally, to trust Him. He wants relationship. Before Jesus, people had to sacrifice lambs, bulls, goats to God to atone for their offenses. That was the law. But then and now, people tend to wander away from God to do their own prideful thing, which is never a good thing.

"Then He gave us Jesus, the very Lamb of God, His own Son, as a perfect sacrifice for us. A torturous death on a cross! For you, Mom. Our sins aren't just atoned for; they are totally forgiven, all of them, once and for all, because Jesus paid the ultimate price with His perfect life. No one could doubt the miracles surrounding the life of Christ. When they buried Him, they couldn't even keep Him in the grave. No, He rose out of the tomb three days later, fulfilling prophesy of the coming Messiah. Do you know where He lives today?"

"In the church?"

"Well, yes, but more accurately, His spirit lives in His believers. It's His spirit in me that you see and want. Do you believe what I'm saying is true?"

"Yes." Mom did not hesitate, nodding her head as she answered.

"Then let's pray and thank Jesus, who just came into your heart. He has given you eternal life with Him."

The event changed the rest of her life. She called me just days later to report that she had zero desire to drink alcohol. She couldn't understand why, but she was absolutely delighted. No more talk about Socrates. At ninety years old, she was a babe in Christ and receiving the blessings He had in store for her. He was changing her, sanctifying her.

Wow, to witness my most long-standing prayer answered after nearly thirty years! Only God could have known the holy praise that burst from my heart for Him. And what boundless grace that He allowed me to be part of the sacred moment!

Mom had a bad accident not long after when she fell again in the night, broke bones, was hospitalized, and was never again able to return to her independent living apartment. Osteoporosis plays hardball in very advanced years. Months went by, and assisted living followed rehab. None bode well with her.

"Get me out of here." The call came from Mom in the middle of the day on a Wednesday. She wanted to move to Denver, right now. All the way to Albuquerque, I prayed while driving that the Lord would give me enough time to help Mom know Him better before He took her home.

Lord! This is so big for her to decide on her own. I didn't even suggest it. But clearly, You are leading this. There is no other explanation.

She's never lived in Denver, leaving her beloved Albuquerque after thirty-two years. I'm the only one she knows in Denver, and I'm not exactly her favorite kid. It's cold up here compared to where she has lived for so long. But compared to Montana, well ... Her circles of friends may have dwindled because of advanced age, but still, this must be so scary for her. O Father, I just pray that she will know You much better before You take her home. What can I do to help make that happen?

I confess I'm worried—You know me so well; I don't have to tell You. Please don't let me get out ahead and try to control because I'm fearful. There's a lot of risk in everything about to happen, meaning I'll need You every step of the way, starting now.

Thank You, Jesus, for this! Mom will go to church. She will meet Christian sisters she didn't even know she has. For the first time in both of our lives, we are going to get to know each other really well. How do I thank You for making this happen?

I drove up through Raton Pass and into New Mexico, sharing my scattered prayers with Jesus, my friend. Coming over the highest elevation of the pass, beginning the descent, I rounded a familiar curve and looked out over the first wide panoramic view of the high desert. Shock would best describe the impact of the scenic beauty unfolding. I immediately steered into a roadside area designated for scenic viewing. In all the frequent driving of the road, never had I witnessed anything so stunning.

Near sunset, clouds played with in-and-out light, using sun and shade like a moving paintbrush. Light bathed soft-pink, orange, red-and-yellow blankets, while ground shadows of the shifting puffy clouds toyed with desert contours of many unique plateau-topped land islands, dotting the wide horizon. All the exquisite detail took place under a gigantic, flat horizontal cloud formation through which light pierced like a colander. The beauty caused my little world to stop to experience an unrestrained release of heartfelt awe. I believe the Lord winked, so to speak. His glory in the display of such a scene could not be denied. No one else was stopping on the highway, so I thanked Him for such a glorious personal showing blessings in store for my mother.

Mom and I spent her last chapter together—very meaningful time for both of us. We grew close. Yes, she had dementia, meaning her mental capabilities were steadily diminishing. But she was still the mom and person I knew for the entire time of the degenerative disease. Initially, I placed her in a nice assisted-living residence that was within a couple of miles of my residence. Her sight and hearing were so diminished, doctors explained to me, that at best she might still have 10 percent of the failing senses. Living with me was not possible while I still needed to work.

I had always known Mom had a critical eye, as it were. She didn't mind telling you that you had a problem. She might be diplomatic about it or she might not be, depending on who you were. Or she didn't mind voicing a personal problem she was having that didn't seem right or just to her. In fact, she could camp on an issue until it changed—the controlling thing. This was not the same mother I brought to Denver.

Bible stories were the answer to my prayer that the Lord provided for Mom to know Him better. My idea to do a Bible study of Philippians morphed quickly to something else the first time I tried at her new home. Only one of the twelve attendees sitting in a big circle owned a Bible. She asked me to locate a certain book she could not find. The book was Genesis.

This was a captive group, all women, so I shifted gears asking if they would like to hear the story about the man God used to write the book of Philippians. When they all agreed, I turned the pages back to Acts in the Bible, which was lying open on my lap. Mom had done all the inviting from her dining room, new friends of about two months. Seated right next to me, she was wearing earbuds connected to a small two-by-three-inch box in my jacket pocket. Mom could hear every word I said, as I spoke into a very small microphone on a cord that connected to the same device called a Pocketalker. She was ecstatic to understand so clearly since hearing aids had long been abandoned.

I told the story of Saul of Tarsus on the road to Damascus and his conversion to the new man we would know as Paul. From time to time, I would reference the Bible for validity, but I knew the story well enough to tell it, not read it. For the first time ever, I was a storyteller! Alive, animated, and able to engage my listeners, they wanted to hear more when I finished. For nearly an hour, all of the elderly stayed fully awake, most having been given their evening medications, which famously cause drowsiness.

Yes, I was a new face, new activity to attend, fun presenter, but mostly they were fascinated that the story I told was true and came from the Bible. They wanted to know more about the Bible, more about the Lord. Especially my mother. I found great joy in the new gift I had received, a gift grounded in our Creator and a partnership with Him in meeting the needs of these sweet people.

Bible stories were weekly; most of every book of the Bible has many. Preparing for them was nearly as much fun as telling them. I was deeper into the Bible than I had ever been, looking up original-language meanings for keywords and researching cultural background for many of the characters. The group size grew, and attendees were faithful. I loved watching them connect with one another in ways they had not otherwise, caring and sharing. Prayer time grew richer. The time came when Mom's needs exceeded the care offered and we needed to seek a new residence.

"I will only move here if you allow my daughter to tell Bible stories," Mom told the administrators of the two places we considered might be a good choice. Only one agreed, making the decision easier for Mom. The new place would have been my first preference for a host of other reasons as well, but allowing Mom to make the choice was important. Folks hated saying goodbye to Mom, lots of tears and prolonged hugs, but they were quite stern in telling me I was not allowed to leave. Now, I told Bible stories in two places. In the midst of all of Mom's care and trying to keep the business alive, our little family was about to change. Hanna was getting married. Her decision to marry was such marvelous news, and the man of choice was well worth the wait. Both were forty, never married, different in many ways, but shared values in important things of life. Their love for each other was as transparent as glass.

Mom was not able to travel out of town for the wedding, so Hanna dressed in her gown in Mom's small assisted-living apartment. I watched Mom's frail fingers slowly move all over the satin wedding gown, "seeing" the beauty of her granddaughter in a grand showing for just one. Mother made me promise to journal every detail of the event.

Serving

" **W**hat are you doing?" My friend Luann leaned into the table we shared at lunch one day, as I told her Mom was growing so interested in the Bible through the stories I was telling.

"I can't believe you've been doing this for more than a year!" she responded. "Goodness! It's been too long since we caught up. Is anyone else working with you?"

"No, I wish. I'm into the second facility, and twice a week is quite a lot. I love it, but I'm still trying to keep a business going."

"Annie, this is multi-housing kind of work you are doing. You need to be a part of our ministry, and you could receive the help you need. Plus, prayer support and fellowship with others. You don't need to be alone."

"Where do I sign up?" I asked my friend who headed up the multi-housing ministry at my church. "And please don't tell me I have to come to meetings."

"You'll get a lot more out of this than you realize." Luann's smile was loaded with confidence. "Yes, there are meetings, but they are also prayer meetings. You will love the others you'll meet and to be part of something bigger. Just come next Wednesday morning and see what you think. I already have someone in mind who might want to work with you."

That fast, I was part of a ministry with outreach purposes much bigger than my own, and Luann was right. I got more out of belonging in my church ministry than I could have realized. So did Mom. Though she was never able to physically participate beyond hearing Bible stories, she loved feeling included and hearing about successful outreach efforts in other assisted living residences and in apartments. The woman who Luann had in mind to help was also an answer to prayer. Lindsay breathed fellowship. She was infectious. She added a whole new dimension to Bible stories, and they loved her. It didn't hurt that she was a prayer warrior.

Mom's first residence was in such close proximity that daily visiting was easy. Often, I would sit with her during dinner with others and stay until her bedtime. But residence changes occurred four times as her need for care escalated. Her second place was farther and, in rush hour, traffic more involved, but still doable daily.

The third was quite a distance, but different. A residential home located in a residential neighborhood, a home converted to care for five patients, this was an environment where her need level was more ideally addressed. They had no problem with my telling Bible stories. It was becoming the one constant in Mom's life, apart from me. Her limitations meant that taking her out for church or other things she enjoyed was very infrequent.

Mom had strong preferences, opinions, memories, and so on. They grew less strong, but she retained her own identity to the end. The amazing part of her very last life chapter was she changed—changes she had something to say about, apart from dementia. I never saw her moody or depressed despite the huge takeaways occurring. She was never demanding, critical, complaining, anxious, or frightened, with the exception of a brief stage of hallucination. I wasn't with her every minute, but the caregivers reported the same behaviors I was observing. The things that genuinely delighted her were far from her former world.

Alcohol was history, she loved the Bible, and church was a weekly highlight for as long as she could go. She had very little interest in material things. Oh, she still loved to laugh. Her disease stole her ability to walk, find the right words, shower herself, dress herself, and do some of the most basic and personal things we want desperately to do for ourselves. Her functional losses were staggering, even feeding herself and speaking at the end.

She never complained, and we never even mentioned the word *dementia.* Mom was still with us. For example, after three years of telling Bible stories, I found myself in a time crunch one week and simply did not take time to prepare a new story. Instead, I pulled out one of the earliest stories. As I took Mom back to her room afterward, she reached up to pat my hand pushing the wheelchair and told me she had enjoyed the story even though it was a rerun. I was thrilled, shocked!

But the biggest shock was that she knew her kids to the very last. This was not characteristic of the last stages of any dementia. Why the Lord allowed her protracted death of vascular dementia, I didn't understand. God didn't owe me an explanation. He knew what He was doing, and I had learned to trust Him. The most amazing thing about Mom was that I believed *she* had a handle on this at some level. Never complaining! Her faith was evidenced in her trust in Him. That was pretty amazing! She did the hardest chapter of her life with grace, with style, with Jesus. I will remember my mother as my hero.

As the business demands diminished, the Bible stories grew right along with Mom's needs. While I might have needed the income a full-time job provides, the Lord saw things differently. Additionally, I had been absent too many years from my beloved HR world to be welcomed back with open arms. Not in a dynamically changing field even on a part-time basis. Doors were tucked closed tightly, despite the prayer support of friends praying for God's very best will.

"Why don't you consider doing the senior ministry here at Green Valley Church? Bob is retiring next month, and we will need to replace him," Senior Pastor Luke said to me in the parking lot one day. He made the suggestion following an inquiry about the success of my job search.

Shocked! I didn't even have to think about my answer before saying, "Because I'm not qualified." Actually, I secretly pitied the poor soul they found to replace the giant Bob who had become a legend before he even left the job he held for thirty years. A deeply loved legend!

"The Lord does not call the qualified. He qualifies the called," Pastor Luke said. "Bob didn't go to seminary. The Lord grew him in the work he loved. Think about it, pray about it. And it won't be the same job. We are breaking it up. Some of the staff will take on some of the responsibility. We want to replace Bob with a part-time person."

Driving away, prayer began before the first red light on my way to Mom's.

Jesus, I admit it would be wonderful to get off the church prayer request list. But seriously? I can't believe any amount of prayer is going to result in hearing You say "follow Me" to that job. Bob's job! Part-time or otherwise. I'm flattered that Pastor Luke would even say that! Please, Lord, You already know I will need an income shortly, like very shortly.

Part-time would be ideal given Mom really needs me, and Bible stories are only getting bigger. I can live on less, which it seems I'm already doing. I would certainly consider something outside the familiar HR world, if You think my skills will transfer. Well, that was silly to say! Every job You have ever put me in I was not qualified for! Transferable skills? Oh Lord, You will have to purge the HR language out of me.

And please, Lord, can we call the cleaning business retired? It has limped along nearly five more years than I thought it could after the stadium. Not that I'm ungrateful because I'm not. I thank You for this business! It has been incredible, as much ministry as business. You knew way ahead of me that Mom would need me, that Hanna would be getting married, and I would become involved in the church ministry. I would not have the time for a full-blown business right now.

I love my life actually! You've blessed me beyond words. You have faithfully led me to every day of work in my life. Even delivering newspapers. I know You have plans, and the timetable is Yours. Please help me wait patiently, to keep my eyes and ears open to the next door You would open. Let me not get so distracted that I could miss a thing, Lord!

Sleep was lousy that night. Pastor Luke's statement about called and qualified bounced around all night, pounding out new corners in my brain. I was on a train going nowhere, and the conductor called the names of only the qualified to get off at the stops. My name was never called. Fear of being stuck indefinitely on an aimless train finally woke me. Half asleep, I was figuring, *Pastor brought the whole thing up just to be nice to someone too long on the church prayer list. Oh no, folks are feeling sorry for me.*

Then I thought, *Maybe I misunderstood altogether—the meaty part of the job is going to staff, and the part-time position left would be basically support.* The night was much too long, and now I was fully awake with the dawn. Standing at the coffeepot, I knew I had an appointment with the Lord in my quiet time that might look more like an interview.

Good morning, Lord! I'm especially grateful for all new mercies this morning! I love Your promises! Thank You for coffee; my brain is working. O Lord, did You put Pastor Luke up to that conversation we had in the parking lot? That would be just like You. And, Lord, should I not know by now that You will never lead me to a pessimistic thought? Please forgive my quick dismissal, fears, and self-serving thoughts. So let me again begin by thanking You this morning. Thank You that You brought me out of Egypt! I am Yours! You have performed miraculous things over and over in my life. I will remember! I praise You Lord today and always.

You have equipped me for everything You have asked me to do. Never was I qualified for the work I have been paid to do or for volunteer work either. Goodness! I came to serve, not to be served and honored to be able to say that. Yesterday, I was invited to throw my name into consideration to serve as a part of my church. Goodness! Thank You for the lousy night's sleep, I might have missed such a gift altogether or at least been too late to respond. Whatever the work may be, I know You have used the godliest man I know to open the door to me. Thank You, Lord Jesus. Of course, I will follow You wherever You lead.

In Your name I pray. Amen.

For four years, I was blessed to serve on my church staff. Part-time or otherwise, they were the best working years I would have. I did not have to walk in the footsteps of my predecessor, just try to walk in those of Jesus. To serve with like-minded, like-spirited, like-hearted people, who share ultimate goals to edify our Lord, was a gift I never imagined I would receive. A monthly highlight was working with our own senior volunteers as we served lunch to about two hundred seniors in our community.

The best part was about building relationships with our seniors, either serving with them or helping with their needs. We played together, some planned and some spontaneous. We shared burdens, prayed together, and belonged together. I was part of the knitting together of the Lord's people for His purposes. Nothing could be better.

Mom was really what led to Bible stories then senior ministry at church. The panoramic spread of beauty the Lord shared with me at the top of Raton Pass had come to pass. My prayers were so much less than a very big God delivers.

Stella was a faithful attender at one of the assisted-living Bible stories, but was losing strength and health in her nineties. She loved the Bible stories, and one day stopped me with questions that followed illustrations I had given to bring an old story to present day relevancy. Her questions kept coming until we were hopelessly down a bunny trail talking about African orphans and widows, culture differences, the devastating effects of AIDS in Uganda where my friend was a missionary, and Christianity amid witchcraft. My efforts to pull us back to the Bible story were interrupted one last time.

"Annie, you need to go tell Bible stories to the seniors of Africa!" Stella announced.

So that's what I did a couple of months later. Praying prayers like, "Lord, Your will, not mine, I'm all in, or I'll follow You wherever You lead," may require a passport and vaccinations when He answers.

Mom was status quo when I decided I could make the two-week trip. In fact, when I told her about the plan to go to Uganda for seniors, to tell them Bible stories, she squeezed my hand. Her degenerative disease had taken her words, but she didn't need them to bless my intentions. Seeing her the last day before leaving was a special time. She liked when I would do her hair or bring something sweet to eat that I made at home. I did both. Before leaving, I prayed with her and loved on her with hugs and snuggles. Goodbye was sweet. I didn't know it would be the last time.

I learned Mom went home to Jesus when the trip was half over. Of course, Pat was like a sister with the very best kind of support as she delivered the news. African women have experienced many times more death and loss than most American women can imagine. I was to experience comfort from compassionate arms unlike any other. I also knew I didn't just *go* to tell Bible stories; I was *sent*. Finishing the short mission was important. Processing and grieving would hold for a few more days. Mom would have been very pleased that Bible stories would be heard a few more times by some who might not ever learn what she understood best—that it's never too late in life to find Jesus. So I told the rest of the stories for Jesus and for Mom.

The airplane ride home was an improvised sanctuary, much like when the ancient Hebrews pulled the prayer shawls over their heads and drew close to the Lord.

Lord, thanks to You, Mom is finally with You, a baby in Christ at ninety years of age, a blessing that surpasses any words to match in gratitude! Please, Father, hear my heart. I rejoice that she is with You today! Goodness, I can't imagine what might be happening for her right now. Unending joy in Your presence, connecting, worship, celebration, seeing Dad and other family, perfect life! How do I thank You that I can know and experience the comfort such knowledge brings, both her salvation and Your timing in taking her home?

Yes, I would like to have been there with her, but I know Your wisdom prevailed and there was purpose in how and when You took her. You have answered fervent prayer that her death not be protracted any longer at the age of ninety-six.

Vascular dementia would seem unending in both loss and length. She has been leaving us a little at a time, hence grief began a long time ago. Still, gracious as Your answer is to prayers, just five days after You took her home, I'm front and center at Your throne, both praising You and needing the comfort I believe You reserve for huge grieving. I did not anticipate this. I'm absolutely thrilled You have my mom, that she has You, but I'm broken without her.

Please, Lord, fill this oversized hole in my heart before I try to fill it with all the wrong things. You know me well. I feel handicapped—I don't know how to go forward without her. Please light my path, Jesus. Amen.

The prayer and many similar fragmented others were repeated in chaotic progression, more like bursting popcorn, during the twenty-four hours of lengthy flights from Kampala, Uganda, to Denver, Colorado. Uninterrupted time with the Lord can be a rich blessing without wireless device usage. Assigned seating means just that—stay put. I doubt the Lord minded being sprayed in tears and prayer, but my end of the effort grew exhausting.

Feelings were complex. *Joy* was big because I knew where she was at long last. *Relief* for her sake, her extended arduous death journey was over. *Love* for the woman handpicked by the Lord to be my precious mother. *Proud* of her, she certainly finished with grace, a child of God for only six years. Yet as advanced in age as she was, her life was clearly changed, evidencing she submitted to the Lord, fully trusting. *Grateful* the Lord answered the prayer uttered for more than a year to take her home. Ninety-six years old, in late stages of vascular dementia, she had no remaining visible quality of life. The disease had ravaged her body.

I felt great *comfort* that Hanna had stepped up in my absence to stay with her when death was imminent. She even sang to her grandmother with the voice of an angel. Even my sister came to see her and might not have had I been there. *Empty* was moving in fast and taking control. No one ever replaces Mom. Gone now, the reality that I'd never see her again was a miserable emotion I had not anticipated. *Lost* and *alone* slammed right into empty. I really, really didn't want to make her death about me.

Guilt was not a feeling in the mix. I followed the Lord's will to take Bible stories to seniors in a remote rural part of Uganda. From biblical characters, I was able to give biblical encouragement to Ugandan seniors who were culturally disrespected and many abandoned as having outlived their usefulness. The very money needed for the short mission trip was supplied by the seniors in my church family. The Lord was in control—all of her days were known to Him before even her first began (Psalm 139:16, paraphrased). All means all. It has a sum total, a finite number. He alone knew I could not be in two places at the same time.

A change of focus brought immediate *peace*, as I pictured Mom in the arms of Jesus, able to walk, see, and hear once again. What awesome, powerful images the Lord provides in His comforting presence!

No, we are never lost or alone. It's okay to miss her, I thought as I felt physical pain in my heart. *How can I feel peace and pain simultaneously?* Tears flowing, I turned to gaze out the window and experience the *grief* in store—I just lost my momma. Only Jesus could fully get that.

"Not alone," I heard resounding in my mind not long before coming into Denver. While it wasn't exactly the answer to my questions, I knew the Lord's unmistakable presence had responded. And I didn't really much like His answer, so I was reasonably certain I had not answered my own question. Maybe He meant going forward with a roommate. I already had a dog, so apparently, Marnie didn't count. No, I knew exactly what He meant. Married twice with disaster endings had been more than adequate motive to move me into an airtight hidey-hole for ten years, locked into my permanent resolution to never remarry.

I had a wonderful male friend, seventeen years older. He studied the Bible, read widely, led others in significant ministries, and was a fabulous conversationalist. I was blessed and marveled that he also benefited by our friendship. We shared nearly every Friday morning breakfast for years, which was more than meaningful in terms of male company. Our time spent together had a profound influence on my Christian growth. I loved the man-friend.

The Love Story

The Lord's leading had begun on a jet ride home from Africa. Sad to say, I took three months to take the first tentative step to follow Him.

Dating websites were evolving quickly by the time I clicked open my first in 2011 on a promotion weekend of "*free* for the looking." *Free* was hardly my motivator, but the Lord knew I would not pay money to put my first big toe into the dreaded dating scene. Mental repetition of "not alone" was the short leash He was using to pull me out of my hidey-hole. Three months of resisting was nothing to the Almighty Matchmaker. Christianmingle.com saw me coming.

The programming in these dating sites was more intricate than schematics for a space shuttle and stickier than West Texas asphalt in August. I must have left footprints all over the site from the first time I touched my mouse. The dating website was quick to show many men I was supposed to want to meet. By the end of the weekend, I was fully affirmed that all good men in the world were married. Certainly, nothing these guys in my computer said was true, and I figured the photos were at least ten years out of date. Christian Mingle flooded my computer monitor for the following week with men the dot-com was certain would interest me. Not!

As time passed, I knew my attitude was raunchy and my spirit was

180 degrees from obedient to the "not alone" message still speaking to me. I love the Lord and also fear Him, so I looked at another Christian website. My trust in the second one was worse than the first, so I returned to the original site, trying again to respond to my Lord.

But now I had to join, meaning not only did it cost money, but I also had to answer a host of very personal questions. As I continued apprehensively to click my way forward, I considered having just one small glass of wine—well, not for long and not seriously, but goodness! This was nothing short of quicksand torture in my mind.

When hyperventilation tried to jump-start my next move, I pushed back from the computer. *Nope! Not one more fearful click with sweaty palms, out-of-control nerves, and me at the helm! I know what it feels like when the Lord leads. Not this. Time out! Time to pray, to listen to the Lord, not myself, to turn to His Word. Just do it! Submit my will, my control, my fears to Him.*

His words told me exactly what I needed to hear. "Whether you turn to the right or to the left, your ears will hear a voice behind you, saying, 'this is the way; walk in it.'" (Isaiah 30:21). He taught He would leave me with his Peace, not as the world gives. Not to let my heart be troubled and afraid (John 14:27).

Walking with God had patently shown me that praying His Word has profound effects. How could He possibly bless my efforts even though I was trying to do what He asked? My attitude was a showstopper. Immersed for several days in His Word, I realized obedience placed me in the sweet spot of the Lord's will—no safer place to be. It was no coincidence that the sermon preached that Sunday was about living in God's will. Perhaps not the easiest or most comfortable way, but definitely the safest. Returning to the computer, I gave it my best effort.

Working for God, not men (Colossians 3:23), I told myself. The words were still fresh in my mind. Answering personal questions was no longer the arduous struggle that had me in an aerobic sweat. Occasionally, I wondered what other women had written in their self-descriptions, but of course, I did not have access to their narratives that might have helped to model my responses.

Writing with the same transparency I would appreciate receiving from a man I might meet, I revealed who I was—my faith, things I enjoyed doing, some of my goals, and opinions. Questions about my preferences were easy; that was up to the Lord. But the geographic question needed my attention. Not only did I intend to remain in Colorado, I also did not want to search more than a few miles for someone compatible who loved the Lord. I complied with the requested recent photos. Once the required profile was completed and membership fee paid, pushing the final button was truly an act of obedience that felt good.

I was free to search within the entire national website, although my interest remained in my immediate geographic area. The website quickly determined numerous possible matches and sent them back. I opened each profile prayerfully and carefully, as each person was a possible answer to prayer. Many did not want to reveal much about themselves. Others were less guarded but revealed desires or beliefs that conflicted with my own.

Twice I agreed to meet for coffee. One of the coffee dates lived in Colorado Springs, which I eventually decided was entirely too far away even if he were a Paul Newman lookalike with a heart like John Baillie. He was neither. It didn't take an hour with him to figure out God was in his backseat, not driving. The other coffee meet lived in a world of complicated expectations of the perfect woman he had been mentally evolving his entire never-married life. I left the coffee shop having been given a reading list of books and articles he said would be foundational in our budding new relationship.

Ben was first to receive God's prompting, slowly widening his search beyond his comfortable Houston base, responding in unconscious obedience to the familiar nudging of His Father. The retiring pastor, recently widowed, told others he believed he would have to go some distance to find the woman the Lord had for him. He had dated a few women in his area, but no one really turned his head. At first, he expanded his search from fifty to one hundred miles, then three hundred, then five hundred, and eventually one thousand miles—reaching Columbia, South Carolina; Phoenix, Arizona; Miami, Florida; Chicago, Illinois; and Denver, Colorado. Circumstances continued to affirm and strengthen his understanding of the Lord's will as he reviewed hundreds of women's carefully prepared self-descriptions and photos. Many responded to him. God was stirring a man of bold faith, bold nature, bold and unconditional love, a man not easily detoured. He stopped on the screen with my face and read a description that was unlike others. Later, he would say he recognized a love for the Lord that was akin to his own. He described the "call" he received at that moment on the same scale the Lord used thirty-two years earlier to call him from the church he pastored in San Angelo, Texas to start a new church in Houston. He believed his search for a woman was over.

Late one evening, I logged into the dating website. A little wiggling icon of a head bobbed up in the lower right corner of the computer screen, a message the dating site program sends in saying a man was interested. A Texan had seen my profile and wanted to take the next step.

"Texas!" I said out loud and blew it off quickly with a click. I might only have been doing this for a couple of weeks, but I was more certain than ever I needed to stay in my lane, My-Little-Niche, Colorado. And the name he assigned himself for anonymity of cajanpreacher! A firm confirmation we lived in different worlds! No, different planets! *What on earth am I doing in a dating website?* The thought just rolled in like gravity pulls on anything free-falling, causing a little more effort to dismiss than merely clicking away the distraction of a bobbing icon. *Stay focused*, I reminded myself. *This is where I belong.*

One thousand miles of distance between two people may mean nothing to the Lord, but it was dense fog for me. I couldn't see the Lord in the little icon in the lower corner of my computer as Ben made his first approach, or the second, or even a number more. I was too busy seeking the Lord's will, not a persistent odd man from Texas.

Finally, after several days, I opened his profile, more annoyed than anything. Opening the file triggered all kinds of programming things in the dating website I would have no idea were happening, including a message to Ben that I was also interested in him. I decided, *The prudent, kindest thing to do is to send a message to whoever this persistent peculiar man is, "you need to go away."*

So I wrote a brief message that said, "May the Lord bless your efforts to find the woman He has in store for you." To a man on a mission with a single focus, this was all the affirmation he needed. My message was a come-on. Ben's next step: he had just two questions about things I had written in my profile. Not sure why I answered, but probably figured the cool brevity of my answers to the inquiry should seal the not-interested message. To Ben, my second response was a solid, "Game on!"

To my brevity, he wrote freely and he wrote well, showing he was articulate, and knowledgeable. Surprised, I thought, *You're not at all like the men I'm communicating with, focused on making coffee dates. Okay, so maybe you aren't so peculiar, but you really need to change your cajanpreacher handle.* He got my attention. At least he was interesting. Our exchanges continued.

My justifying thoughts were, *What's the danger in sharing biblical opinions or heroes of the faith with someone clearly intelligent and so very far away? He doesn't even know my name. This guy might know more about the Bible than anyone I've ever met. I love his testimony of how he was led into pastoring. There was no way we are ever going to meet, even for coffee. Besides, if he really knew me, this man would never be interested in me. This can stop at any point. No harm done, no one hurt. Hmmm…surely, this person couldn't be very serious about someone living one thousand miles away. Cajanpreacher, you are biding your time with me while doing a focused local Texas search, just like I'm doing in Colorado.*

Meanwhile, Ben was turning up his Texas charm. I was beginning to look forward to his next reply. His questions and answers were relevant, so our writing grew lengthier as subject matter broadened. He recommended we switch from the dating site to standard email so we could send photos and links. Sharing our email addresses and names was really not that difficult to accommodate. But with the change, I began to sense I was treading on risky ground. I could not deny this was a person of interest. We were both invested.

The first serious thought crept in that the Lord might be behind the ongoing connecting, not just a website programmer. Really scary thought, but quickly rejected! The possibility of Texas moving closer to Colorado was zero. Sooo why was I participating in a go-nowhere, very intriguing online don't-know-what-to-call-it thing? Probably because it was far more engaging than anything in my geographic area.

The nagging feelings grew stronger. Time to stop the pointless communication, the foolishness. Whatever was happening was quickly moving out of control. No money had been spent, and the only investment thus far was time. Perhaps Ben sensed my growing uneasiness, or maybe he was doing his own sanity check.

Almost immediately, he announced he planned to visit his sister in Colorado Springs and her husband. Soon. Would I have dinner with them? In a flash, whatever had been happening to that point, catapulted to a whole-earth orbital level. I was spinning with thoughts I could not connect but turned them to prayer.

> *Oh Lord, to say no is going to be very difficult, but why? I don't want to hurt this good man and realize I have been leading him on. How incredibly selfish and insensitive of me to not be thinking of the consequences. There is way more invested than just time on his part, not only mine. Of course, emotions and heart count! Probably more than money. What have I done?*
>
> *No, wait! Isn't he leading me on, Lord? He's the one who came after me, that little bobbing head from Texas in the corner of my computer that wouldn't go away. He's been pulling me in! Who did this? Both of us? Oh Lord, what*

part are You playing in all of this? I'm so far over my head!
Please help!

Ben did not wait to hear back from me before sending his next message. He thought it would be appropriate that we finally share phone numbers and talk before we invest any further in making a decision to meet. That seemed reasonable on one level; I could end things. It might be a kinder thing to do while talking with him rather than emailing. Or at least postpone a dinner invitation answer. Or he may say something that would give me a good honest excuse to say, "No, thank you." Or he may not like me.

On another level, hearing his voice could change everything. If the Lord were in this, would I not need to keep things open until I knew for certain? Justifications mounted to take the next step and speak with him. As the phone rang, I paced and my heart raced as I said a flash prayer.

> *Lord, I pray You will protect this man from me. And*
> *please, Father, protect me from him. Your will, not my own,*
> *I ask. In Jesus's name…Amen.*

"Hello, Ben."

"Hello, Annie." He spoke in a smooth, heavy Texas drawl—deeeeep, gentle, resonating, a beautiful, mesmerizing voice. Never had I heard such a voice or my name that way! I was completely unprepared. In just two words, he delivered all the control he needed if he were to lead me over the rim of the Grand Canyon. I returned from my planetary orbit to a no-posture seated position in my soft living room club chair, totally settled and at his mercy.

Our conversation lasted nearly four hours. Everything about it was easy. The man was a trust-me magnet. Questions and answers were all based on truth—a mutual desire to be open and transparent. We shared a deep love for the Lord and agreed He was probably a part of what was happening. If ever my fears were disarmed, it was in those moments on the phone.

Ben was demonstrating respect and trust in me while leading the way in meaningful conversation, rich with the Lord's presence. We shared stories of our weaknesses and the strengths we had found in Jesus. The topic was cause for confession, disclosure of past and present difficulties, and even some laughter. We spoke of the gifts He had given us, our passions, and callings. Of course, we talked of our families, personal things like aging, health, lifestyle, and places we had lived. We each listened.

Every day for two weeks, lengthy phone conversations delved into those things that mattered most to each of us, and we both found God at the epicenter of them all. We began to marvel out loud at God's presence in our developing interest. His church's website made finding what I wanted easy—his Sunday messages. Goodness, he was good! A teacher more than a preacher, incredibly easy to listen to, and he was not afraid to go deep into God's Word.

Talking with him was a different world—a place of tender acceptance, comfort, and amazement. I revealed difficult things I rarely talked about, like the fact that I had been married and divorced twice. His questions were compassionate, heartfelt. Responses were often biblical, reminding me once again that I was speaking with a man who was firmly grounded. He shared in more detail how the Lord had called him into ministry, how he was called later to move from San Angelo, Texas, to Houston to start a new church. He described knocking on twenty thousand doors and beginning the church in his home, then moving to an old convenience store. He talked about the prolonged illness and death of his wife.

Soon, Ben expressed the "investing" shouldn't go any further until an actual face-to-face meeting occurred. I agreed. I asked if he would be willing to speak by phone with my pastor before coming to Colorado. He agreed. Finally, we broached the topic of Colorado and Texas. He bought an airline ticket to Denver.

As much as I felt the Lord's presence in the uncharted waters of a budding new relationship, when I would hang up or shut down my computer, I felt a cold wash of doubt and fear steal my contentment. Self-talk didn't take long to turn harsh, even critical. *This person is nine years older. Perhaps that wouldn't be so significant if we were both younger, but our senior lifestyles are also different. I eat healthy, Ben eats Texas fried. My heart is strong, Ben had a heart attack twenty years ago and a couple of stents in recent years. I walk daily; Ben doesn't. Maybe he's looking for a caregiver wife.*

Our physical differences inflated the nine years in my mind. Doubts deepened.

And then there was the Texas-Colorado pink elephant that hadn't exactly gone away. Yes, we had discussed the one-thousand-mile residence difference. It was Ben's intent to retire in Colorado. My skeptical thinking could only see the countless things that could go wrong with that idea! I would try to talk very honestly with the Lord.

> *Smack in the center of my frontal lobes, Lord, is my defeating checkmate—"My batting average in two marriages is zero." Ben's only marriage lasted fifty-three years. What in the world am I doing? What is he doing? He doesn't really know me. When he does, this thing is headed for a face-plant. But then, Lord, the next time connecting with him by phone never fails to move me to a new and even hopeful frame of mind—one that feels very much like You, Lord, are leading.*
>
> *I like this man very, very much. O Lord! Please lead.*

"Pastor Luke!" I spoke his name with a little more volume than intended as I burst into his open-door office at eight thirty the next morning. Startled, he abruptly swiveled his chair around from his computer terminal toward me, wide-eyed. "I need a huge favor. It's personal!" Bypassing all the normal morning pleasantries, I blurted out my mission still standing in his doorway.

I had been working in my church for four years, but my choice of words took the matter out of church business. "This is really bizarre!" I began. "I've met a man, well…no, we've not actually met…a Texas guy wants to come to Denver, and I'll be having dinner with—"

"Wait!" Pastor Luke coupled the word with rapid hand gestures to stop me midsentence. "I'm still stuck on your first words. You are dating?"

"Not exactly, but well…yes, I guess you could say," my uncertain response stumbled out.

"I'll be!" Pastor Luke stalled for a moment on his response. "Go on. But first sit down." I took a deep breath in the brief break and realized what a poor start I'd made. The rude interruption confessed, I started over at the beginning, where the Lord first told me, "Not alone." The story unfolded while my pastor of nearly twenty years, and now my boss, listened well.

As I painted an emotional picture of vacillating hopefulness mingled with well-founded fears, I realized I was pouring my heart out to one of the few men I'd ever trusted. What he would say would have a big impact. No coincidence that Pastor Luke and Ben were both pastors from Texas!

"You're right, Annie, because this is really bizarre, along with a number of other reasons. It's quite possibly of the Lord." He agreed to speak with Ben and assured me that it would not be too difficult to get a reference on mostly any pastor in Texas.

"Here's the website of Ben's church. Maybe you could listen to one of the sermons." I handed him the little wadded-up piece of paper in my hand. When I left, I knew deep down in my knower that my pastor had my back. Far more had occurred in the hour than simply a requested favor granted. The Lord was smack-dab in the middle.

My children didn't know I was into a dating website, much less the extent of involvement with one man that I hadn't even met. I shared with Andrea, of course. She raised questions and concerns, many I couldn't answer. "One step at a time." She offered her wisdom. The only other person who knew what I was doing was the woman now working with me in Bible stories.

Lindsay was gifted in relational ways that enhanced the impact of the story told and helped bond the listeners with one another. I had grown more than fond of her. One evening, as we walked back to our cars, I felt moved to share the bizarre thing unfolding. She stopped me in my tracks, took my hands, and began praying to the Lord that He protect me and make clear His wisdom and guidance in the matter. Her prayer was certainly effective in drawing me nearer to the Lord, but I had no idea how important the intervening prayer would be in the days to come.

"Ben Blest is pure gold," Pastor Luke reported a few days later when he called me to his office. Not only had he called Ben, but he was also very pleased with results from the call. The do-you-know-who portion of the forty-five-minute conversation yielded at least five people they both knew. Pastor Luke knew them well enough to call them. He explained to me the relationships and more detail of what he found, especially the person who used the analogy of pure gold.

"Have you heard of Texas Baptist Men?" he asked.

"No. Do we have a Colorado counterpart?" I responded.

"Oh, not exactly, but TBM trains volunteers in many other states to do what they do in disaster relief. They have been around for forty-five years, about fifteen thousand volunteers today. They are the first people to show up with disaster relief following hurricanes, floods, tornadoes, and such. That's what they are best known for. However, they do far more. They build churches, clean up drinking water around the world, disciple young people, and serve in such a way that others come to Christ. Ben was one of the earliest members. I'm told if you stick him, he bleeds TBM."

Pastor narrowed his eyes as he leaned into his next words. "Ben said he is definitely courting you!" I grinned at the use of such an outdated expression, but a mere grin was my supreme effort to suppress utter elation over such remarkable findings. Pastor had learned a good deal about me in the matter of a few days, but he couldn't possibly know the depth of my distrust of men or lack of confidence in myself where men were concerned. His words were crucial affirmation.

"One step at a time." His final counsel might have been in all caps.

—†—

He rose slowly on the escalator, his profile emerging onto the same level where I waited for him behind a barrier at the busy airport. I had studied the photos he sent, so there was no mistaking him in the moving crowd. I began to smile as the anxious waiting had finally come to a close and a new anxiousness began. He turned his head to search for me. We locked eyes just before he stepped off the escalator. I sent a hasty prayer to a Lord I believed was leading the unfolding event.

> *What a gentle face, thank You, Lord! I love his eyes! Goodness, he's all dressed up in a sportscoat in July! He's kinda beautiful! He's old, very mature, but good mature! Well, I'm old too. Great smile! What on earth am I going to do with him for six days? You're in this, right, Lord?*

His confident stride quickly closed the gap of fifty feet between us. Neither of our eyes moved, even as my anxiousness might have been at a lifetime high.

It was my intent to give him a warm welcome hug. His mind was someplace else. Before I could redirect anything, he bear-hugged and planted a passionate kiss right on my mouth, evidently motivated by Richard Gere in *Shall We Dance*, as Gere made such a bold, heated move with Jennifer Lopez. Instantly, I knew I was not in control. I was experiencing something for the first time in my life, and that's tough to say at a senior age. My sense was my future would not be the same. I pulled away enough to see his eyes again. Deep, rich, bottomless eyes looked back at me. There was nothing pretentious or ungenuine there. Just depth, wisdom, sparkling life, and confidence.

"Well...hello, Ben! Welcome to Denver." When I found my speech, it felt unnatural. I smiled with every ounce of composure I could muster, doubtful I would ever sort out what just happened. I might not be able to control Ben, but I knew I had to gain control of myself.

"Hello, darlin'," he responded then released me and picked up his briefcase. His smooth Texas endearment didn't help my control issues; the words only served to boost my anxiety, which I considered might be nearing a stroke level. Ben's eyes searched the airport for signage—baggage claim. I wasn't helping; I was talking to God.

> Goodness, Lord Jesus! This is nowhere near one step at a time. I just dove off a cliff and couldn't tell You if I were free-falling to my death or airborne in flight to another planet. Please tell me what's going on.
>
> You knew this was coming. Oh, Father, couldn't You have let me know? I know You are on my side—Your Word tells me so, and it is great comfort. But...You are on his side also. Hmmm, that thought confuses everything. Bottom line, Lord, trusting him is so far beyond me right now, and for sure I don't trust me. And You know I'm not ready for the i-word—intimacy!
>
> The moment calls for the right words, and I don't have them. Could You please give me some spirit-inspired words? Please, Lord, just stay in the middle of this, and can we keep this prayer open, please?

"If this is going to work, Ben, I need to ask you to put your hands in your pockets and keep them there for the next six days, please?" The words were far from spirit-inspired. They were terribly clumsy and blunt, but at least I had blurted out some semblance of self-control. The airport was noisy, and a loudspeaker announcement competed with me—he didn't exactly hear all the words.

Thank You, Lord. That was mercy for Ben.

I repeated, but not word for word, taking the additional moments to soften the first terribly awkward reply. Still, "hands in your pockets" came through with, "Let's get to know each other better first." The steady look in his eyes never wavered as he thought about my request then slowly nodded a smiled agreement. We walked to baggage claim, more connected than either of us realized. A great deal would happen before we returned to the same spot.

The Six-Day Date

"Let's pull over at the top of this hill and talk. I have an idea." I spoke in response to Ben's last question while slowing the car and easing off the highway onto a county dirt road. We drove a couple of hundred yards to a wide spot under a shady oak tree and turned off the car engine.

Today was day three of what we would later refer to as our Six-Day Date. We already had a routine. I would pick him up at his hotel, which was only two miles from where I lived, by nine o'clock, then plan our day. Most days closed with dinner at my place. Home cooking was pretty much absent in Ben's life. He didn't even care that he was eating leftovers from the first night's enchilada casserole.

Ben had been deer hunting in Colorado on numerous occasions, so he already knew what he enjoyed most about the state. We spent much of our time appreciating the outdoor majesty of God's creation while sharing ideas and experiences we thought would enhance our ability to know each other better.

The easy rapport we had discovered in the lengthy telephone conversations quickly resumed in person. We boldly asked and answered questions that mattered. We were parked at least 150 miles from Denver on a scenic, high, wide-open mesa, the nose of the car pointed northwest, viewing an unobstructed nearby mountain range with snowcaps still visible mid-July.

We opened the windows and quietly rested in the natural sounds. Grasses were moving around us as a gentle breeze ushered in our next sharing time. There was nothing hurried about the day, especially the moment. A nearby bird eventually interrupted the intoxicating nature spa, chirping for someone's love in the avian world.

"Would you be willing to read aloud something that is especially meaningful to you at this time?" I handed Ben my Bible, which I had placed in the car's console before leaving home.

He held the Bible very carefully, purposefully. The Psalms opened to him as he rotated the binder over in his hands. Turning only a few pages to reach Psalm 147:1–11 (NIV), his deep melodic voice began with the first verse: "Praise the LORD. How good it is to sing praises to our God, how pleasant and fitting to praise him!"

Called to read God's Word! I thought. *Perhaps never have I heard it so full and beautiful than in this present idyllic setting. I am the only one in hearing distance; thousands should be.*

"The words I've chosen direct us to praise a great God, at the same time reveal the Creator, the God of grace and comfort, the intimate connection He designed with His chosen people," he said then continued reading the psalm.

> *The Lord builds up Jerusalem;*
> *he gathers the exiles of Israel.*
> *He heals the brokenhearted*
> *and binds up their wounds.*
> *He determines the number of the stars*
> *and calls them each by name.*
> *Great is our Lord and mighty in power;*
> *his understanding has no limit.*
> *The Lord sustains the humble*
> *but casts the wicked to the ground.*
> *Sing to the Lord with grateful praise;*
> *make music to our God on the harp.*

He covers the sky with clouds;
he supplies the earth with rain
and makes grass grow on the hills.
He provides food for the cattle
and for the young ravens when they call.
His pleasure is not in the strength of the horse,
nor his delight in the legs of the warrior;
the Lord delights in those who fear him,
who put their hope in his unfailing love. (Psalm 147:2–11, NIV)

I watched the gentleman read on to the ending verse 20. All my senses were in tune, taking in, absorbing, thirsting for more. He began reading in Psalm 146, another psalm of praise expanding on the character of God the Father, containing many of His promises for our good and God's purposes. Not certain if my hunger was for more of God's Word or the man reading it, I knew I had experienced something far more intimate than a kiss.

He looked up then spoke from his heart about his love of the Bible. He explained to me in detail how faithful the Lord had been throughout his life, to accomplish His will in many impossible situations. His testimonies rang bells of fulfilled biblical promises, one after another, in his stories of new church planting, missions, and the transformation of lives and his family.

This was a righteous man, one who spoke from a humble place, quick to footnote his stories with his source of all things good. His leathered face reflected the character, love, and promises of God who had carried him a lifetime, working the Father's will. And he was still pastoring, fulfilling his passions. *What was not to love about this man, Ben Blest?* My thoughts were uninhibited as I watched him speak.

"Do you like ice cream?" Ben asked.

"I can't believe you waited until day three to ask me the most important question in my life!" We stopped on our way back to Denver at an old roadside general store displaying an ice cream sign. The log structure had a wide, wraparound, covered porch on three sides. The mountain view on any side was entrancing, but we chose two big Adirondack chairs on the north side to settle into, eating a frozen taste of heaven in the shade.

Ben's phone rang and he apologized, "This is a call I need to take from Joy." Evidently, he didn't need privacy as he remained seated and slipped into an easy exchange of small talk. Once business was completed, they returned to sharing on a more personal level. He described a few of the things we had been doing and then expressed that he was especially enjoying the company he was keeping. Joy evidently wanted to know about his trip and if he was having a good time.

"Joy, I'd like for you to meet Annie." He extended his phone to me.

He had often spoken of her in the context of his church, always with the greatest respect. It would seem she was the quarterback of operations in his absence, maybe even when he was there. She and her husband were both professors and proverbial pillars in the church. My mental image of them was nearest-possible perfection this side of heaven.

If I could have shot him with my best critical look from a gun, I would have. The utterly shocked expression on my face was meant to do the job. Ben didn't flinch. His steady grin didn't either, as he released the phone into my hand halfheartedly extended.

"Hello, Joy! I'm so pleased to meet you. Ben speaks of you often with the highest regard," I spoke and prayed simultaneously she would not hear my seriously lagging emotions.

"And hello, Annie. Likewise, we have heard a great deal about you." Her voice betrayed no shock at the impromptu meeting Ben just maneuvered. "I hated to interrupt your day, but it was something I thought Pastor would want to know. I'm thrilled he has taken time off for himself. He virtually never does. Sounds like y'all are getting to know each other."

"Yes, we are. And we couldn't have picked a more beautiful place to do this." I had no idea what I might say next. I climbed out of the Adirondack chair just to breathe. Ben stood as well and walked away in search of a restroom. Thankfully, Joy took the awkward moment we were given and moved on gracefully.

"Pastor has had a rough time of it since his wife passed. We've all been concerned about him. He doesn't do so well all alone, and I know he has been making an effort to meet a lady outside our church family. He shared with me that he was trying to date, but the ladies he's met here in Houston have not really worked for him. I suggested he try an online dating approach, where he might be more particular, you know what I mean, maybe selective?" Now, Joy was struggling a little. We both laughed nervously.

"I know exactly what you mean, Joy. Online dating is a whole new world from when we first dated, right? It's brand-new to me. I 'computer-met' Ben just two weeks into my first effort. I never intended to connect with someone outside my area. Still trying to sort it all out—how this happened and has come this far."

"When Ben knows what he wants, he moves forward. I've seen it time and time again."

"I definitely get that sense. He's a lion!" Again, we laughed. I had used Dr. Gary Smalley's language, which characterizes personality types as animals—a language we both understood. "It's why he's here, I believe."

"I'm very fond of him," I continued. "Has he ever met anyone who didn't like him?" I asked more as a rhetorical question.

"Oh yes, but that might take us back to Ben the lion." This was followed by more laughter.

I liked Joy. She felt approachable, and I sensed we were into a communication of greater meaning than just first-encounter pleasantries. "Joy, I'd very much like to share openly with you. May I speak from my heart?" Ben had not returned yet.

"Of course!" There was audible relief in her answer.

"I'm finding dating is so very different at our age," I began. "It would seem the games and nuances of younger dating are passé—instead, serious efforts to really know someone happen. Time matters more. I guess we want to quickly eliminate those we discover wouldn't fit. I know that sounds cold, but honestly, that's what Ben and I are doing.

"I really like him, a lot, Joy! But…it worries me a great deal that he could get hurt so easily if either of us discover a roadblock. There's a vulnerability about him that makes me terribly cautious. At the same time, I don't want to be so guarded that I would be less than honest. We've come a good distance down this path in such a short time, and there's no sign of slowing. We both are aware of the Lord's presence. Ben has invested considerable travel money to come here, which is also a concern, but more than that, I would just hate to see him hurt." Logic, feelings, and fear comingled in my expressed thoughts.

"I'm so glad to hear you say this. We absolutely love Pastor and would hate to see him hurt also. He told us quite a bit about you, shared his thoughts and feelings before buying a ticket to meet you there. He truly believes the Lord is leading him, and he's incredibly strong-willed. There was no talking him into slowing down. At the same time, we wanted to encourage what seemed to be a genuine possibility for him to pursue. There is a lot of prayer covering this trip." Joy paused.

"Could we pray together right now, Joy?"

The long-awaited dinner with Ben's sister was planned for day four. It was almost laughable that he didn't even tell them he was coming to Colorado until after he arrived. In his defense, Ben did not lie. He later explained that his careful choice of words in the dinner invitation were, "I'm *planning* to visit my sister."

Shirley and Paul were amazing. It was more like mutual love at first encounter. Paul was an impressive cook, and Shirley was willing to tell me everything about her brother's childhood while Ben vehemently claimed lapses of memory. The evening was quality time with quality people. We had more stories to share than time to tell. We all wished sharing, laughter, and the easy rapport could go on longer. The encounter went beyond serendipitous. I felt like I had met people that I would see again. At the very least, I wanted to.

If these people were representative of the rest of his family, the depth of Ben Blest was very impressive. Time to let my children know their mother was seeing someone. My best friend knew about Ben. I promised her she would meet him before the week was over, which left only one more day.

"I thought you were never going to get married again, Mom!" they nearly spoke in unison. "Where did this come from? Who is he? Why are we just now hearing about this?"

"First, I'm *seeing* someone, I didn't say I was getting married. Second, it's only been a few weeks. It's not like I'm hiding anything." My defenses were strong, and I knew I was off to a poor start. Their questions were understandable, given the short notice of informing they had received. I was nervous. My two adult children, very bright, were worthy of more respect than I was showing. What did I really want to say to them?

Driving home from Colorado Springs the night before, I delayed the day five start time with Ben and invited Hanna and Peter to meet for breakfast. Hanna was still on summer break for teachers, so I found a place not too far from where Peter needed to be by eight o'clock. It was six forty-five when we huddled at a small bistro table in a bakery/café.

"He came all the way from Texas to see you. That's some *seeing!*" Peter challenged right back.

"And, Peter, did you get the part about him being a pastor?" Hanna threw a little ammo to her brother.

"Okay, can we start over?" I pushed my chair back a little and laughed. "I wish I could tell you what I want to tell you, but I'm still trying to figure that out. Meeting Ben was never really planned. I can't even tell you exactly how I feel about him. I just guess I really need your support wherever this may lead."

"Why don't you start at the beginning and tell us how it all happened?" Hanna asked the right question I had been too anxious and defensive to figure out. I very much wanted them to understand what was developing, as uncertain as it was. However, explaining a faith-based event to my prodigal children was like reading every other word of the Pledge of Allegiance. I did my best while they just stared at me, sipping their coffee.

"You can't seriously consider moving to Texas?" Hanna's probing question spoke for both.

"I have no idea where this may lead. Before things went any further, I wanted to let you know what I *do* know. I'm very fond of this man."

"If you don't want to move to Texas, then maybe you better be leading this, Mom." Peter offered sincere advice as he and Hanna exchanged glances and nodded in agreement.

More questions followed. Most centered on our physical and age differences, geographic differences, and speed with which a new relationship seemed to be developing. They voiced concerns and the opinion it would likely fizzle out shortly when logistical reality took hold. They were pleased I had taken steps to meet someone and voiced pursuing local opportunities would really be for the best. They were also pleased that I was including them in what was happening.

Hanna concluded, "Ben sounds like a good man, no doubt, but Colorado has plenty of good men. You don't need to go as far as Texas, Mom. Give your search a little more time. You really just got started."

"Yeah, Mom, you're a good catch. Take your time," her brother injected as we gathered our personal things and gave the table to waiting customers holding hot coffee.

—✝—

Driving to Fort Lupton would take an hour, and the drive would not be pleasant country cruising. I had told Ben that Andrea was the wisest woman I knew, and meeting her was like meeting my sister in terms of importance. It was midmorning before Ben finished emails and phone conversations with people who kept a church running in the senior pastor's absence. He would be home tomorrow.

Our northbound journey had barely started through the inner city in moderate traffic when my right rear tire suddenly went flat. I pulled over quickly onto the shoulder of I-25. There was a wide spot on the interstate shoulder, the highway department built for their use, which must have been the equivalent of three or four lanes in width. We were literally in the shadow of the Broncos stadium that loomed like a high-rise snugged up against the southbound interstate lanes. I pulled the car to safety at the guardrail and called the roadside assistance number listed on my insurance card. The noise dominated as the traffic roared by.

"We have about thirty minutes to kill." Embarrassed, I tried to explain. "Of all things to fail! The tires are the newest things on this car. What on earth caused a flat? They're only three months old!" The day was starting to warm up, so we stepped out of the car and stood close to the car at the guardrail. Soon, we were leaning on the rail, gawking up at the towering stadium separated by at least ten lanes of thundering traffic.

"I can't believe you cleaned that whole thing!" Ben said, close to my ear so that it was possible for me to hear him.

"All 1.8 million square feet, some twice as the trades stacked up toward the end. I partnered with another small company to do the construction cleanup in two months. We still had the contract at the old stadium right next door, simultaneously with the new stadium construction cleanup."

I pointed several hundred yards to the north. "They held rock concerts there nearly every day all summer. Wouldn't tear it down until the new one opened. Plus, we were cleaning up the Denver Coliseum circuses, wrestling matches, and other events. Summer concerts at Red Rocks Amphitheater six nights a week had to be cleaned. And the speedway. Actually, it was a nightmare."

"Where was your husband?"

"Germany on business."

"What did he think this was, a hobby?" Ben was looking at me, jaw tight, eyes pinched narrow.

"I can't believe my brand-new tire went flat right at this spot!"

"How did you get through it all? Tell me the story, please."

"Two weeks before completing construction cleanup of the new stadium, I called Chuck to tell him I could not continue by myself without his help. He needed to come home. He was in Germany on business more and more often, staying longer and longer on each trip. I literally begged him to become part of the business, which was intended to have been his from the very beginning. That wasn't the first time we had the conversation. The original plan had become a sore topic.

"Long story short, the commercial cleaning franchise corporate office believed I was most suited to get a business started and profitable. Then Chuck would move in, take the helm, and I would go back to being happy in my HR world. But Europe came into the picture and grew far more interesting and glamorous to Chuck than cleaning up offices and stadium trash. Turns out so did the European women, but I learned that later.

"He came home, reluctant and angry, driving directly to the stadium from the airport. Found me in what we called our command center, a gray windowless cinderblock room about twelve by fourteen foot. Blueprints of all stadium levels, sections, seating, boxes, restrooms, locker rooms were taped on all four walls in various colors and stages of final cleanup. Status of completion, construction supervisors' approvals received or needed, number and location of our assigned personnel, their leads and supervisors were noted on each blueprint." I explained what the room looked like that Chuck would see for the first time.

"Command center was base for all operations: for radios the supervisors carried, reporting, calendars, all communications, everything." The story just rolled out. Ben was easy to talk with, and this was not an easy topic.

"I was thrilled to see him, like the Marines had landed, though he was not exactly dressed for the job, trained, or happy about being there. The whole scene was new to him, but I wasn't worried. He was there, and I took my first deep breath in months. He was smart and would catch on quickly. I knew I could bring him up to speed enough for me to leave for just an hour. More adhesive remover was desperately needed for signage. Work would stop before more could be delivered. Taking Chuck throughout the stadium, meeting the building supervisors and our own people would have to wait until I returned with the remover. In the interim, everything he might need to know was taped on a wall.

"It was a quick trip. I thanked the Lord all the way there and back for the return of Chuck. The cleaning business was not the only crisis going on. Ben, this was all happening ten years ago this month. My eighty-eight-year-old father, living in Albuquerque, was rapidly failing, both with his heart and a nasty fall that broke his hip. I was making so many quick trips to Albuquerque, my mother forgot I lived out of town. I was beyond exhausted. I needed Chuck in every way."

"I can imagine," Ben said. "Go on."

"There he sat when I returned, in the only chair, feet propped up on a five-gal painter's bucket he found, reading the paperback he started on the long flight home from Europe. 'What on earth are you doing?' I asked him as I walked in.

"His answer? 'I don't like your tone!' he quickly replied as he stood to face me. 'You have no clue what intercontinental flights take out of you or the sacrifices I make for you!'

"Honestly, Ben, I had no idea what to say. I was speechless. It wouldn't have mattered anyway. His mind was made up before he got off the airplane. He didn't want to be there, that was clear. So he stretched to his full height and announced, 'I'm outta here!'

"With that, he essentially walked out of my life. To make sure I understood his intent, he turned as he walked into the concourse and threw the house keys at me as hard as he could.

"Notification came a week later that we did not win the contract to provide cleaning services for the new stadium. Dad died about a week later. My own personal 9/11 happened. My twin towers, Dad and Chuck, came down."

To hear each other, Ben and I were standing quite close, both facing the enormous stadium. Ben had respected my request to keep his hands in his pockets for five days—100 percent. As we watched the roadside service vehicle turn into the wide shoulder, I felt his touch. He had reached out his arm behind me. I felt it on my back, and his hand gently cupped my upper arm.

"I'll take it from here." His words were barely audible. I wasn't even sure I was meant to hear them. I melted. If he knew, he didn't say more.

"The Lord's redemption of everything you just heard is an even better story. You need to hear the best part."

A short time later, we pulled out onto the interstate, tire repaired, and resumed our journey to see my best friend. "The story of Chuck, the stadium, and my dad is a hard story for sure. But, Ben, you probably know even better than I, the Lord can redeem anything, and He did. If we are alive, the story continues. It's about Him, not us."

Andrea lived in the country, east of the mountains. These were flat agricultural acres, dotted with livestock and quilted with crops. The eastern slopes of the Rocky Mountains sprawled the entire western horizon. Widowed for the second time, she remained in the rural community where she had lived the longest. She even still owned a couple of horses.

"My respect has grown tremendously for this man, Andrea," I said at the first opportunity that we were alone. Ben had stepped outside after visiting for thirty minutes to walk a little on the property, feed some carrots to Andrea's mare who had been calling us since we arrived, and probably give two friends a chance to talk candidly about him. He was not insensitive to the importance of Andrea's impressions of him. I knew my time window with her was limited. I posed the crux of my most pressing questions to the most important spiritual mentor I had.

"What makes marriage work?"

"Submission," she responded without hesitation. "First, to the Lord, then to each other. Submission is nonverbal. It's an attitude, a behavior. Don't forget it's all voluntary! The idea of submitting is for the purpose of pleasing the other person, giving preference to the other. Jesus submitted to His Father! He said *all* His authority was given to Him by His Father."

Andrea never failed to astound me. Her wisdom, even when battling cancer for the third time, was so clearly supplied by the Lord. "The Lord designed marriage, giving us each a role. The husband is submissive to the Lord, but he is also honoring his wife. May sound perplexing, but it's not a contradiction.

"The Bible tells us that the husband is head of his wife, he is the leader of one woman. Only one. People who are not believers take this out of context and believe men are to dominate all women. Wrong! The biblical counsel on marriage speaks to believers about authority in marriage, not the worth of the wife or her abilities. It's about authority and accountability.

"Most conflict in marriage is about control. When God's design of authority, selfless love, and desire to please are all applied, a marriage of beautiful harmony can honor the Lord. Only then will the couple experience the full extent of joy in each other that the Lord designed. Our broken world doesn't make this easy, but when we are purposeful, we find our efforts are incredibly blessed."

The wisdom just rolled out of her. "Succeeding in marriage is not about all the things that you share—interests, opinions, and even passions or temperaments. It isn't even if you have experienced what the world touts as the perfect models in childhood. It's about keeping eyes fixed on the model the Lord has set up and honoring each other in every conceivable way life can offer day after day."

When she paused, I said, "So much of the discussion with Ben, even before he got here, has been about the Lord's perspectives of things. But we've only touched lightly on the topic of marriage because, well...I've probably been guilty of avoidance. Of course, he knows my marriage history, but that's different.

"Visiting with him nonstop for five days is hardly about casual dating, Andrea. He didn't come all this way just to find a functional companion. Let's face it: we are investigating whether we might share a love for the other, suitable for marriage. Whether this is the Lord's will and His leading.

"We aren't young. At our age, we get stuck in our ways. Not much flex or change left in us, so to speak." I offered what might be an insurmountable obstacle.

"That's what the culture will tell you, Annie. God's Word tells us the opposite. We *are* changing, transforming, clay in His hands if we give ourselves to Him. There's that submission again! Submission is such a stumbling word, especially for women. The word has nothing to do with superiority.

"The Bible goes out of its way to show us that we are all fearfully and wonderfully made. No one is superior to anyone else, except, of course, God the Father. The only way that the wife or woman is referenced in the Bible as weaker relates to physically weaker. We are *made* differently. She is as worthy of the same grace, respect, and love a man receives. In fact, we're told a husband is to honor her as a fellow heir."

"Andrea, can marriage really be like that? I mean, I feel like I've experienced two of the exact opposite. I don't just fear men! I fear marriage! And I see so many other marriages that fail. You describe something so perfect."

"I had two good ones. I know I was exceptionally blessed. Men who loved God and honored me to their last day. My marriages weren't perfect, but I have been loved."

"So what did you fight about?"

"Oh, we had our arguments. I can honestly say they didn't characterize our marriage. They really didn't happen that often, but yes, we got a taste of misaligning what was important. We all have a nature prone to selfishness. When we promote our own agenda and welfare over others, whether we do it subtly, obviously, or even unknowingly, the Lord will give us all the rope we need to show our agenda. Those are the hardest days that don't have much to do with love. They are the path to apologies." We laughed, each having firsthand experience.

"If you could put it all in a sentence, Andrea, what would you advise?"

"Try to outgive each other and never expect anything in return." Andrea summarized her thoughts, having only briefly met the man in question. She knew me well enough to know we had reached a serious level of relationship despite the short span of time. "Decisions need to be paved in prayer."

"Amen to that! Thank you from the bottom of my heart for who you are!" We were hugging when Ben returned.

The airport trip came too soon. Somewhere in the whirlwind of a six-day date, Ben found the time to prepare a sermon he needed to deliver in Houston the next day. I would have walked him to his gate before the new world of security-driven travel. Once baggage was checked, we had a little time to walk the distance to security before his flight left.

We approached the top of the escalators and moved a good distance to one side. I wouldn't be going farther. Only a brief awkward moment passed, and then without words, we moved together into a hug. As I wrapped my arms around Ben, he held me snuggly. My face lay alongside his chest and shoulder; we fit perfectly. Close was comfortable, secure, beautiful. Feelings of belonging, peace, and utter contentment held me motionless, unwilling to release him. Nor did he even try. We hugged and hugged. I could feel his warm, steady breath on my neck. To the bystanders, we likely stood locked together much like a bronze statue. Truth was the two living people, nestled firmly together, had called time to stop for just a little while, to savor the gift of love.

God's Best

The trip had been on my calendar for three months, in ink. Precious time was growing short, and Eric knew I would come to see him as promised. His liver cancer was stubborn, treatment wasn't helping. His home was a long drive, but I would drive twice as far to see my cousin. The one thousand miles to Kalispell, Montana, began at 5:00 p.m. the day after Ben returned to Houston.

I hadn't reached the city limits of North Denver when the tears began. They continued nonstop until I cried myself to sleep in a motel on the other side of Cheyenne, Wyoming. These were torture tears of regret that simply would not quit. The prayer conversation that brought me to a decision point began with my drive home from the airport. By the time I reached Wyoming twenty-four hours later, I had mentally replayed it ad nauseam.

> *Lord, Ben's a winner, I'm a loser. My marriages end in disaster. My life is full of brokenness, his is beautiful! Doesn't matter what I tell myself or what he says for that matter, I'm simply not in his league. Ending this today will hurt him terribly. On the other hand, to marry him would be far worse, right?*

Yes, I think we will both be hard-pressed to move past this. Whatever pain goes with that I deserve and even more; he doesn't deserve any of this. I should never have encouraged him.

We're not equally matched physically or spiritually. And financially, he's two-thirds and I'm-one third. We're lopsided from any angle. He sure doesn't deserve that I could wreck the rest of his life. All those wonderful feelings we experienced are just feelings. Very misleading, we wanted to believe You were leading, but I connected dots I wanted, not necessarily guidance from You.

I've done that before too many times! You know them all. We hear what we want to hear, and truly Ben was too good to be true. I'm a fool! What have I done?

Just before I left home for Montana, I touched the Send icon to Ben on the tenderest Dear John letter ever written.

The second day of driving was going to be nearly nine hundred miles, and I couldn't get the tears to stop. Ben had sent back an email response to my Dear John letter. Wasn't that just like him? That he would send a sweet response to rejection. Just affirmed one more time the winner/loser perspective. In essence, he told me he heard the Lord's leading in our relationship and also he understood if I had not. Further, *if* and when I did, *if* I felt differently, I should feel free to call him. Goodness! I knew I had hurt a very special man, St. Ben.

For hundreds of miles, conflicting thoughts continued to rivet back to Ben despite my best efforts to launch new thoughts. The radio, snacking, phone calls to the kids—no diversion worked for long. It was like he was the wallpaper of my brain. Justification efforts for what I had done would not sweep away the guilt thoughts.

I did the right thing—he's nine years older. Our physical fitness differences are greater than nine years. I eat healthy foods; he eats whatever is fried and not on a healthy heart diet. I walk; he watches football.

Negotiating one thousand miles between Houston and Denver would require huge sacrifice no doubt. Can he live apart from his roots, or can I leave my family, small as it is? One of us must.

He's not just a pastor; he's also a theologian. At best, I'm a Bible storyteller and spiritually ordinary as vanilla ice cream. He has devoted his life to the Lord. My life looks more like a road map for what Proverbs warns against!

He's such a winner, he will be snatched up by a good woman in no time. His pain will be short-lived.

Sending the letter really was the kindest thing I could do.

So why was I still crying? I felt worse, not better.

It was great to see Eric. So, so sad he didn't look great. The visit was about Eric. So much to catch up. Just being with him and his wife Sandy pushed the mental wallpaper aside. A terminal disease erased all pretenses from conversation, no magic in that! No one really cared when they ate or sleep; visit time was open-ended quality time, transparent time. Love was freely expressed. Naps taken when needed. We laughed and cried, shared, and prayed. Eric knew exactly where he would be going shortly; he had no fear. Confined to a chair and bed for quite a while, he discovered TBS on television and favored a few great pastors. Not a big reader, the Lord reached Eric via television. He filled him up.

Before leaving, I briefed Eric on the rapid rise and fall of my Ben chapter. "Your logic is flawed." Eric didn't sugarcoat his opinion when he wore his big-brother hat. "God will take care of Ben—that's not your job." Wasn't hard to hear the wisdom in that! How I was going to miss this favorite man in my life. He lived a simple good life.

"Do you think God might see this match as lopsided?" I asked.

"Stop!" Eric cut me short. "I'm going to give you back your own words of counsel. You told me not to compare myself with others to determine my self-worth. That's biblical, sister."

"Well, this is different," I bounced back. "We're talking possible marriage."

"You say you are seeking God's will, but honestly, all I hear is justified fear." Eric laughed, knowing he had fully exposed me. "You set God aside when you take over like that. You really need to figure out what fear has you so paralyzed. You won't hear God until you do." His wisdom hung suspended in the air like a sunset can, which brings us to focus entirely on what the Lord intends.

One day had stretched to five in no time at all. No planning or self–pep talk can prepare us for a last goodbye with someone we love. Crying began again while driving, this time for Eric and the goodbye that Sandy would soon be saying. If crying while driving were illegal, I'd be doing life in Leavenworth after this trip! Jesus cried more than once. Hundreds of tear miles for Eric, then the Ben wallpaper returned. My tears nearly always led to prayer.

> *Lord, I can't miss the irony of going one thousand miles in the opposite direction from Houston. Two thousand miles away from Houston, this is starting to resemble Jonah's rebellion that got him a three-day ride in the belly of a fish. When fear overcame Your man, he took matters in his own hands, running a great distance in the opposite direction from Nineveh, running from You. Is Houston my Nineveh?*
>
> *What am I doing, running? Eric was spot-on! Fear is my motivator, my driver, my worst enemy! I sent the letter to Ben in a fear seizure.*
>
> *Yes, Ben will be snatched up quickly, but, Lord, what if her intentions are not all good? He's such a righteous man. In a refreshing way, he impressed me as somewhat naïve in the ways of this horribly broken world. He just doesn't live here like most people do. But like Eric says, You will take care of Ben. Please, please protect him! I ask in Your name, Jesus. Amen.*

Second-day driving was Sunday morning in big-sky country, meaning I was in the middle of gigantic, open land stretching in all directions under vibrant blue skies dotted with occasional little white cotton balls. Majestic panoramas. Signs of people, towns, or even other cars were infrequent. A radio station broadcasting John McArthur grabbed my attention. Understanding what he was saying was another thing. Lousy reception turned five minutes of choppy voice/static into a weapon of temptation to swear at the radio. The remote location spelled nothing to be gained by trying to find another broadcast.

Refocusing on the breathtaking visuals on all sides brought my heart and mind back together, making a natural transition to begin praising the Maker of all I could see. Shortly, praises became audible! I thought, *Oh, why can't I do church in the car? I can sing, pray, maybe preach a sermon to self on my favorite scripture, Romans 8:28.* I sang a song by Michael David O'Brien.

> This is my story, this is my song
> Praising my Savior all the day long.
>
> Blessed Assurance Jesus is mine
> Oh what a taste of glory divine
> Heir of Salvation, Purchased of God
> Born of His Spirit washed in His blood.
>
> This is my story this is my song
> Praising my Savior all the day long.

I sang the words to the Lord, worshipping from my heart, knowing my journey with Him was our story, His and mine. *The fact that I can't sing doesn't matter to the Lord. He gave me one note. I just haven't found a song yet that has it.* Like prayers, our singing praise is worship and fellowship with Him, which did wonders for me and delighted Him. He drew me closer. I kept singing, this time a song by Laurie Klein.

I love You, Lord and I lift my voice,
To worship You, O my soul, rejoice;
Take joy my King in what You hear,
May it be a sweet, sweet sound in Your ear.

Keenly aware of His presence in the car, I might have begun another song or prayer if an impulse to cry out to Him for wisdom had not taken me to another direction. The need for closure with Ben was overwhelming, at least between the Lord and me.

Oh Lord, only You know what a mess I've made, how I have hurt someone so dear and just how much. Please, have mercy on him and tell me what You would have me to do. You are wisdom! I am desperate for Your omniscient wisdom, please! You invite us

My little flip-top phone startled me, lying in the seat next to me as it began to ring. Nothing fancy about the phone except it displayed the caller ID in a tiny lit window as it rang. It said "Wisdom." Good thing I was in the middle of nowhere as my eyes were riveted on the phone, staring wide-eyed for who knows how long. Eventually, the friend's name Lindsay Wisdom came to mind. A split second before the ringing stopped and before running off the road, I grabbed it.

"Lindsay! What in the world are you doing calling me at nine thirty on Sunday morning? Why aren't you in church?" The questions were more or less fired at her. There was a pause on the other end as I'm sure my response was bigger than an expected simple "hello."

"Um, I didn't feel great, probably coming down with something, decided I needed to stay in bed. Just thinking about you, knew you would be traveling today and thought I would see how your trip has been." In addition to working together in Bible stories, Lindsay and I also served together on a pastors' prayer team that always met early before Sunday's first service.

She could not have understood the surreal shift I was experiencing. To move from baring my heart to the Lord to actually seeing the prayer requested for wisdom answered on the ringing phone in the midst of asking, to unexpectedly be talking to another person in the worship sanctuary of my car. Still, I knew the Lord was as present in the phone call as He was in my prayer and worship time. The call was no interruption.

Lindsay Wisdom was a friend with a strong heart for prayer. She was one of only three who knew about Ben. The Lord was using her in a powerful way to answer the prayer just barely spoken. Until that moment, she knew only a little of my recent dating effort. Now, I told her everything. This sweet friend was a flawless listener as I spilled all the chaos, the events, my logic, and overwhelming feelings. I confessed my inability to sort out my own heart's desires from the desires the Lord gives us.

"That you are even dating, isn't that God's leading?" she began when I finally took a deep breath.

"Yes, but—"

"What's with the buts? Listen to yourself! What happened when you had a flat tire? Goodness! The very location of the flat tire that never should have gone flat is too bizarre. Coincidence or chance? Just recently, when Pastor Luke got involved and happened to know key people who knew Ben? A thousand miles away! Coincidence or chance? What kind of references came back through the most trusted man in your life?"

Lindsay was concise as she laid out three points of evidence that the Lord was consistently working in the midst of what I had described as a mess. "*You* told me all of this. I'm not making it up! Girlfriend, is God in this or not?"

And she didn't even know the most recent appearance He made when I cried for wisdom and He used her, her name to answer. Wrapping my brain around that one would probably take more days than I had left to live.

"Didn't he tell you to call him if you ever felt differently?" Lindsay asked after a few moments of thoughtful silence.

"How can I call him, Lindsay? My every thought is how to undo the hurt I've caused. To do further damage a phone call might make to this precious man is the last thing I want to do. I don't trust myself with thoughts at this point, much less actions." Breaking emotions mingled with my words.

"But if I'm listening right, you are in a very different place now than when you sent the Dear John letter to him, right?"

"Probably," I responded tentatively.

"That was not an empty offer he sent back. If you are confused, you are hearing too many voices. There's only One voice you need to hear—the voice of truth. Now ask the Lord and *listen* to what the Lord says."

Her wise words were addressing some of my fears, exchanging some confusion with wisdom, affirming what Eric had just said. God was leading me out of a risky quagmire of doubt onto holy ground in the multiple ways He was manifesting Himself, and I knew it.

"If you decide to call Ben, write down what you need to say before making the call. You have described a very strong man, and it's critical everything that needs to be said gets said. You need to have peace about this whole thing no matter what you decide."

From the time I left Ben at the airport, the overriding thing I experienced had been fearful chaos. I hung up with Lindsay. I knew that something considerably beyond me was happening, both settling and enormously exciting.

Thoughts turned to the possible odds of everything that was happening. *I recently read there are over three hundred prophecies from the Old Testament that Jesus fulfilled. The odds of one man fulfilling just eight of the most straightforward prophecies are one in 100,000,000,000,000,000. When God does something, it would seem He wants there to be absolutely no mistake His work is supernatural.*

What were the odds of my car's very newest part, a tire, breaking down in front of the stadium at the only wide spot on the busiest interstate highway in Denver, at the very location Chuck walked out of my life? Remembering what Ben said at that place, that he would take over from there, still sent chills up my back. The fact that I was even entertaining thoughts of yet another man for the rest of my life? I couldn't speculate the odds. Just knowing I was experiencing supernatural things had all my attention. No, better put, the Lord had all my attention beyond the events that were unfolding. He stirred my spirit to prayer.

> *Lord, Who am I that You would touch me with such grace, such personal inimitable care, such meaning? Why me, completely undeserving of Your unmistakable supernatural work? You are nothing but love.*
>
> *You are perfect, faithful, trustworthy. Nothing in my life has happened that You have not restored and redeemed. Amazing! Over and over, You have shown me that Your ways are not my ways. You have changed me. Clearly, Your ways are always the best, so is Your timing.*

For several hundred miles, I drove quietly. Listening. Pondering what was unfolding. Thoughts would often turn to short prayers, but mostly, I listened. I recalled a favorite scripture. "When hard pressed, I cried to the Lord; He brought me into a spacious place. The Lord is with me; I will not be afraid. What can mere mortals do to me?" (Psalm 118:5–6).

What a contrast from all my self-talk about not trusting men, others in general and myself most specifically. I was so bogged down in my circumstances, my fears, and myself that I was drifting away from what mattered most. *Trust Me*, stuck in my head. I knew the Lord was speaking.

Many sermons and countless places in the Bible speak to us about trusting God. While I probably thought I was on the good side of believers who trust Him versus those who do not, I was sadly mistaken. Trusting Him was firmly ensconced in my head, not so firmly in my heart. Actions told the real story—my trust thermometer—continually begging the question, am I following all He asks? I had just witnessed the profound trust Eric placed in the Lord. The peace he had. There was no pretending. I was so grateful to know where he was headed, that he was a child of the King.

Lord Jesus, Thank You for walking with me, holding my hand, answering my prayers, for Your incredible patience with my pitiful struggle to fully trust You. Just when I think I do, You are faithful to show me otherwise. I want to trust more fully. Please don't give up on me yet. I'll need Your strength to trust You much more.

Thank You for stirring the heart of Ben Blest. For stirring my heart. Thank You for the most incredible man I've probably ever met. Your doing! He's truly amazing! I was so worried about hurting him, I stomped all over the best gift You could have sent to me! I'm really not so different from Mephibosheth, when David restored to him all that he had lost. What a great story You bring to mind!

The poor crippled man yanked out of his secluded hiding place and suddenly at the king's feet was unable to accept the beautiful grace David laid before him!

"What is your servant, that you should notice a dead dog like me?" he asked (2 Samuel 9:8). I know the story well. I've told it more than once.

Forgive me, Lord Jesus, meeting Ben is no accident, no one to reject because I don't deserve him. Which I don't! No one to reject because my fears are so great they would paralyze me. No one to reject because I didn't trust You! He is from You!

I just wouldn't connect the dots because I couldn't believe the goodness of all that was happening. Unable to accept a gift of grace from You! O Lord, what have I done? I sent the gift away! Please, please forgive me.

I have done more damage than I can imagine. I have no excuse, only a deeply repentant heart. In the precious name of Jesus, I beg forgiveness.

Please take these broken pieces and do with them what only You can do, what I've seen You do so many times already in my life! In Jesus's name, for His sake, and for the sake of Ben. Amen.

What's peace? I began thinking. *Well, it's not just the opposite of chaos, though it's that too. When all the counsel is done, when I've faced my own demons and fears, when I stop the pointless efforts to trust myself or even others, when I set emotions aside and listen to just One voice. Only One. The voice of truth, like Lindsay said.*

When I released to God all my fears, fretting, and attempts to control, when I could say, "Lord, have Your will, not mine," then I knew the peace that passes all understanding. Holy peace was God's gift to me. There was no question when I received His peace. Jesus personally delivered His promise. "These things," Jesus said, "I have told you these things so that in me, you may have peace" (John 16:33). My day of worship and the profound encounter with my loving Lord had brought me closer to Jesus than ever before in my life. I felt His love in ways never experienced before.

Whatever guilt might have been eradicated before I arrived home surged back like an emotional tsunami when Ben didn't answer my phone call, letting it roll to voicemail. Good thing I followed Lindsay's counsel and journaled my thoughts before I even tried to speak with him, even before I unpacked. I was too tired to sort through the emotional wreckage from one lousy failed phone attempt, nor did I care. My emotions were nothing I could depend on. God's truths were not part of my emotional pitches. I needed to put them to bed. Trusting the Lord to bring His promised new mercies in the morning, I crashed on my pillow for much-needed sleep after the holy drive home of a thousand miles.

Morning light brought immediate new perspectives when Ben did not return my requested call. The "no answer or response" underscored just how deeply I had hurt him. He was likely receiving wise counsel from others, helping to protect his heart from further assault. Wise man! Still, I felt like a dirty, smelly rag, holding a bag of truth that Ben needed to hear. Whether we ever spoke again or not, knowing the truths would go a long way in healing a wounded heart. Bottom line, I knew what was happening was something much bigger than my guilt, bigger than me and bigger than Ben. Following the Lord's lead, I would somehow get the truth to Ben.

I climbed out of bed, brewed some coffee, and sat down with the Bible and my Lord. Morning manna, new mercies, prayers, drawing closer yet to the Lord—the absolute best part of the day! Closing my quiet time with Him, I prayed once more.

> *Lord, thank You for being the anchor of my life. For giving me life through Jesus Christ. For the truths You continue to provide. For the rich trip. For a brother as precious as Eric. Please receive once again the continual prayers for him said in the drive home and again this morning. For a safe arrival home. Your Word has been a lamp to my feet and a light for my path.*
>
> *Please saturate me more deeply with Your words of wisdom, Your love. Fuel me today on the path You light. May I go boldly knowing my confidence is in You, not myself. Guard my heart, mind, and soul that I will edify You in all that You have equipped me to do. My greatest desire is to bring You my thank offerings—to please You. To do Your will. Please hear the song of my heart this morning … On Christ, the solid Rock I stand, all other ground is sinking sand.*
>
> *I'm fully convinced You have made Your will known to both Ben and me. In the powerful name of Jesus, I give You all my thanks and requests. Amen.*

Taking the journal notes made only twelve hours earlier, I began to expand notes into the form of a letter, to mail the words I would have spoken had Ben answered the phone the previous night. Writing was easy; I was confident the Lord was leading. I didn't wait for routine mail to pick up at my place. Instead, I drove to the local post office, kissed the letter, and released it in the mail slot.

Time followed to wait, trust, and pray.

Lord, You know best that my life journey is so radically different from Ben's. Yes, much brokenness but remarkable works of Your healing, Your rebuilding, not my own, and countless victories won only through You. When I just see me, it's such a pitifully poor picture, a mess. But when I include You in the picture and what You have done with my fragmented life, I'm beyond amazed at Your work.

When I have given my broken pieces to You, Jesus, You fit them together like gems in a complex display of beautiful parts in motion, ever turning to reveal exquisitely cut sides. When Your holy light shines through the many different gems, they are not only beautiful to the beholder, but also irrefutable evidence of Your love, Your power, Your presence. Your Glory!

In this totally unique perspective, I'm a walking love story of Yours. A holy kaleidoscope! O Lord, Ben could see that, couldn't he? That's the attraction! Thank You for wallpapering my brain, for showing me truth, for displaying Your powers and intervening, for forgiving and showering grace all over me.

How I would love to return to the hug in the airport! I would never let him go. But You already know that. I know You have begun a good work in me, and You will complete it (Philippians 1:6, paraphrased). Is Ben to be part of Your bigger picture?

Ben and I both love You passionately. We want to share Your love with each other, with others as we serve on Your behalf, to join our stories for Your purposes. I fully believe You have given me this desire of my heart, so I offer it back as a prayer request. I ask if this is Your will, in the power, the love, and the name of Jesus. Please grant this desire. Amen.

The letter arrived in Houston three days later. Ben called. We spoke for seven hours. His phone had melted on the dash of his truck, and it took three days to replace. He welcomed me back like the parabolic father received the homecoming prodigal son, showering me with the very same genuine kindness, no questions asked. Pure grace! My holy kaleidoscope life turned once again to reveal exquisite holy light amid radiant color, moved by none other than God's grace and mercy.

Our phone call cemented our commitment to the Lord at the epicenter of the relationship and to each other. We knew we were looking at an arranged marriage. A long engagement seemed pointless at our age and given the certainty of the Lord's will. Still, we needed confirmation of His timing, not ours. And our children needed to meet their parent's new intended spouse.

Out of the blue, unsolicited, I received a call from a friend wanting to know if I had considered the possibility of leasing my condo. Her mother was moving to the area in about three months, and my location and home would be ideal. The request was amid a depressed housing market. Ben and I set the wedding date for two months later and arranged weekend trips to Denver and Houston to meet family.

The church was full. When the choir finished singing, "We Are Standing on Holy Ground," Ben and I stepped forward. All *wow* words were exhausted by the time we stood facing those who had come—family, friends, and Ben's church family. Each of us held a microphone to share our side of the powerful God story that had brought us together.

Ben spoke more to me than the congregation. After a few minutes, he invited me to speak also. Together, we took turns telling all the pieces of a journey that brought us to an altar, a story extraordinary in how the Lord worked in spite of us, why we believed He would do this, His timing, and His speed.

Every aspect of the story revealed His omnipotent nature and love. He alone was the Author of an unfolding beautiful love story He intended for us to have each other. Speaking about His handiwork, we were humbled to be the object of such a Designer, for we were not young and the world might look upon our arranged marriage in a very different way. We were especially honored that Pastor Luke officiated the wedding.

I wish I had reserved just one word for the day. One word from all the words I've ever known. A word never used before the wedding day! A word of gratitude so precise, so grand, so enormous, reflective, accurate, so perfect to tell a perfect Lord what I felt for Him at that moment.

My gratitude was definitely for the gift of Ben, but it wasn't just Ben. Hanna and Peter were two incredible children He had given to me, and He was about to expand family in an unprecedented new way. I would need my Lord's constant help not to worship the gift. Nothing worthwhile would be happening without the best of all gifts—Jesus.

This wedding day seemed like the top of the mountain, the highest altar in my life to take all my praise to God—the Giver of all things and who made all things possible. No best words left. Not here on earth. Heaven would be full of perfect new words.

I knew a joy, way beyond the sum of *all* my words, to join this precious man in marriage, serving him and serving our Lord with him.

Epilogue

The title of this book emerged five minutes after Ben's passing. The Lord gave me the image as I stood in the summer morning sun on our front porch. When we give our broken pieces to Jesus, He will fit them together like gems in a complex display of beautiful moving parts, ever turning to reveal exquisitely cut sides. When His holy light shines through the many different gems, they are not only beautiful to the beholder, but also irrefutable evidence of His love, His power, His presence. God's glory! Not everyone sees God's glory, and not everyone seeks it. Ben did.

The Lord blessed Ben and me with nine years of marriage before taking Ben home. Years that were unquestionably the most meaningful in my life, and Ben said likewise because of the transforming that occurred during our precious time together. Remarkable changes that could not have occurred otherwise. Nor should His amazing grace have surprised either of us, for we were the first to proclaim we had an arranged marriage.

But we *were* surprised, again and again. The Lord just does that! Oh, we were incredibly blessed to travel, spend treasured time with family, and build beautiful things in Ben's woodwork shop for family and missions we supported.

The changes that occurred in us and through us during our marriage were made by the loving hands of our Lord. We experienced Him and knew Him far better in divine ways in our years together. I will forever praise such a gracious God.

Blake also passed away. I believe he is with Jesus because he truly was a lost lamb. I can only praise a merciful and wondrous Father who is true to his word that "his sheep listen to his voice; he knows them, and they follow him. He gives them eternal life, and they shall never perish; no one will snatch them out of his hand (John 10:27–28). Many prayed the Lord would open his eyes, his ears, his heart before his last breath. While unresponsive on his deathbed in the last few hours, Blake opened his eyes wide for twenty minutes, grew teary, then closed them. There is nothing the Lord cannot redeem, no one is beyond His reach, and He is gracious to show evidence of who He is so late in the life of one of His own.

Jesus has saved me in every conceivable way. He has been my strength, my best friend, my Abba, healer, restorer, my *everything.* He alone equipped me for an incredible journey with Him. A story to be shared. Time is running short in our world, darkness increases as Jesus, the Light, is returning soon. There are so many who don't know who He is. They do not know that God passionately loves them.

May we all be bold in sharing the Light we have. If we are submitted to the Lord, we are changed. If we are changed, we are a catalyst for greater purposes than anything we can imagine or understand. May our sharing change other lives!

His Word tells us, "But you are a chosen people, a royal priesthood, a holy nation, God's special possession, *that you may declare the praises of him* who called *you* out of darkness into his wonderful light" (1 Peter 2:9, NIV; italics are mine). "Now to him who is able to do immeasurably more than all we ask or imagine, according to his power that is at work within us, to him be glory in the church and in Christ Jesus throughout all generations, for ever and ever! Amen" (Ephesians 3:20–21).

Annie Blest

Printed in the United States
by Baker & Taylor Publisher Services